THE BEDFORD SERIES IN HISTORY AND CULTURE

Confronting Southern Poverty in the Great Depression

The Report on Economic Conditions of the South with Related Documents

Edited with an Introduction by

David L. Carlton
Vanderbilt University

Peter A. Coclanis
University of North Carolina at Chapel Hill

BEDFORD/ST. MARTIN'S   Boston ♦ New York

For Angelo and Alex Coclanis and Emma and Sam Carlton

For Bedford/St. Martin's
President and Publisher: Charles H. Christensen
General Manager and Associate Publisher: Joan E. Feinberg
Developmental Editor: Louise D. Townsend
Associate Editor: Richard Keaveny
Managing Editor: Elizabeth M. Schaaf
Production Editor: Anne Benaquist
Copyeditor: Cynthia Benn
Indexer: William Fletcher
Text Design: Claire Seng-Niemoeller
Cover Design: Richard Emery Design, Inc.
Cover Art: Marion Post Wolcott. *Mrs. Lloyd, ninety-one years old, and daughter with pellagra, in doorway of old log house. Near Carboro, North Carolina, 1939.* Reproduced by permission of Lee Wolcott.

For information, write: Bedford/St. Martin's, 75 Arlington Street, Boston, MA 02116 (617-399-4000)

ISBN: 0-312-11497-4

Acknowledgments

Editorial, Textile Bulletin, July 7, 1938. Reprinted by permission, Billian Publishing Co., Atlanta, Georgia.

Editorial, *Louisville Courier-Journal,* August 16, 1938. Reprinted by permission of the publisher.

Fitzgerald Hall, Frank Porter Graham Papers, Series 1.1, 1938, Folder 70.

Acknowledgments and copyrights are continued at the back of the book on page 163, which constitutes an extension of the copyright page. It is a violation of the law to reproduce these selections by any means whatsoever without the written permission of the copyright holder.

Foreword

The Bedford Series in History and Culture is designed so that readers can study the past as historians do.

The historian's first task is finding the evidence. Documents, letters, memoirs, interviews, pictures, movies, novels, or poems can provide facts and clues. Then the historian questions and compares the sources. There is more to do than in a courtroom, for hearsay evidence is welcome, and the historian is usually looking for answers beyond act and motive. Different views of an event may be as important as a single verdict. How a story is told may yield as much information as what it says.

Along the way the historian seeks help from other historians and perhaps from specialists in other disciplines. Finally, it is time to write, to decide on an interpretation and how to arrange the evidence for readers.

Each book in this series contains an important historical document or group of documents, each document a witness from the past and open to interpretation in different ways. The documents are combined with some element of historical narrative—an introduction or a biographical essay, for example—that provides students with an analysis of the primary source material and important background information about the world in which it was produced.

Each book in the series focuses on a specific topic within a specific historical period. Each provides a basis for lively thought and discussion about several aspects of the topic and the historian's role. Each is short enough (and inexpensive enough) to be a reasonable one-week assignment in a college course. Whether as classroom or personal reading, each book in the series provides firsthand experience of the challenge—and fun—of discovering, recreating, and interpreting the past.

Natalie Zemon Davis
Ernest R. May
Lynn Hunt
David W. Blight

Preface

Several years ago, in the course of work on other projects, the authors encountered for the first time the National Emergency Council's *Report on Economic Conditions of the South.* Its existence was scarcely news to either of us; the controversy over the *Report* is a standard part of the chronicle of modern southern history, and the phrase with which Franklin Roosevelt introduced it ("the Nation's No. 1 economic problem") is a common slogan among commentators on the American South. But the original document had been out of print for well over fifty years, and surviving copies were difficult to locate and consult.

After finding stray copies in second-hand bookstores and reading them through, we regretted the *Report*'s unavailability even more. As longtime students of southern economic (under)development, we were struck by the comprehensive manner in which the *Report* catalogued the deficiencies of southern life, not on an abstract theoretical level but in the most human terms. Moreover, we believed that republishing the *Report* with commentary and supporting materials illustrating the economic, political, and intellectual milieux in which it was imbedded could serve a broad range of purposes. By making it accessible, we could provide undergraduates with an important learning resource and supply other scholars of the South with a critical but hard-to-find basic document. With this, the end product of our labors, we hope that our readers, be they beginners, professional scholars, or educated laypeople of the sort the *Report* originally sought to reach, will find that we judged rightly.

In researching this project we had help from several manuscript repositories and librarians. We would particularly like to acknowledge the assistance of the staff at the Franklin D. Roosevelt Library at Hyde Park, New York, particularly that of Robert Parks; Wilson N. Flemister and the staff of the Archives and Special Collections Department of the Robert W. Woodruff Library, Atlanta University Center; Marice Wolfe and her staff at the Special Collections Department, the Jean and Alexander Heard

Library, Vanderbilt University; David Moltke-Hansen and the staff of the Southern Historical Collection, The Library of the University of North Carolina at Chapel Hill; and Robert Anthony and the staff of the North Carolina Collection, The Library of the University of North Carolina at Chapel Hill.

Various colleagues graciously read the introduction at our request: Otis L. Graham, Jacquelyn D. Hall, William E. Leuchtenburg, John Shelton Reed, Bryant Simon, and George Brown Tindall. We were granted penetrating and useful reviews from the readers for Bedford Books: David E. Hamilton, William A. Link, Michael O'Brien, Bruce J. Schulman, and Thomas E. Terrill. Charles H. Christensen, Louise Townsend, Niels Aaboe, Anne Benaquist, Cynthia Benn, and Series Editor Ernest R. May have made working with Bedford Books an extraordinary pleasure. We also wish to thank William H. Fletcher for doing the index.

The documents presented in this collection have been edited minimally to approach facsimile form as much as possible. Some minor changes have been made in punctuation and spelling, chiefly to clarify meaning or make the documents easier for modern audiences to read. Otherwise the documents have been rendered as they were written. Note that this editorial policy entails the retention of such archaic practices as the use of the lower case in rendering "negro"; the editors do not endorse this practice, but retain it here for historical reasons.

David L. Carlton and Peter A. Coclanis

Contents

PART ONE

Introduction: The *Report* in Historical Perspective

Whether of southern origin or not, Americans today might well have a difficult time believing that the South was once defined in part as a uniquely poor region in a land of plenty. Those who have grown up during the glory years of the so-called Sunbelt, in particular, might find it surprising, even a little implausible, that a bit over fifty years ago the South was called "the Nation's No. 1 economic problem" by no less an eminence than the president of the United States. However surprising or implausible the statement might seem in 1995, Franklin D. Roosevelt was on solid ground when he made this observation in June 1938 in the presidential letter accompanying a once famous document, the National Emergency Council's *Report on Economic Conditions in the South*. The *Report* set forth in clear and powerful language a hardscrabble world that we have largely, if not completely, put out of mind. In a brief compass it laid bare, as the editors of *The Nation* put it,

the facts about the wasting of the South's splendid natural and human resources, the erosion of its soil, the crowding of its rural slums, the draining of its youngest blood and best talent, its ramshackle housing, its starvation wages, its monopoly of pellagra and its subjection to syphilis and malaria, its sparse schooling, its exploitation of the labor of women and children, its dependent farm tenantry and brutal-

1

ized and impoverished landowners, its untaxed industries and its tax-burdened common people — in short, the grotesque paradox it presents of a land that "is blessed by nature with immense wealth," yet whose "people as a whole are the poorest in the country."[1]

The original *Report* was short (sixty-four pages), divided succinctly into four-page, leaflet-sized sections, and generally designed for mass dissemination to a population lacking in verbal sophistication but hungry for understanding about their plight. The language was transparent and simple, accessible to people gathered in mountain hollows, on plantations, in schoolrooms, and at small-town discussion groups all over the region. Its implications were fought out in newspaper columns and in "town-meeting" debates broadcast over the relatively new medium of radio. It spoke to southerners about the hardest facts of their lives, in language they understood.

If the *Report* provides a window through which we can view the southern economy and society before World War II, it likewise allows us a glimpse of southern politics and intellectual life in the New Deal era. The *Report* was a document generated by political appointees within the Roosevelt administration, officials who conceived it in part as a tool with which to achieve political ends. It was also a document generated by southern liberals, members of a loose cohort of like-minded souls concerned about southern welfare and heirs to a generation of thought about southern ills. Finally, it was a document whose long-term impact was limited in ways that themselves tell us much about the transformations that overtook the post – World War II South and the larger nation. Both in its content and in its context, then, the *Report* is a document of pivotal importance for understanding the creation of the modern South.

FIRST GRAPPLINGS WITH SOUTHERN POVERTY: CIVIL WAR TO THE GREAT DEPRESSION

Poverty in the American South had deep roots. From the beginning of southern history the region's plantations had relied on a force of laborers — first white indentured servants, then black slaves — who, not being allowed to own even themselves, were desperately poor indeed. Moreover, at least by the nineteenth century, those numerous southerners who were neither masters nor slaves lived lives that outside observers found pinched and deprived. Even so, the plantation system, mobilizing

[1] "Southern Waste Land," *The Nation* 147 (August 20, 1938): 169.

slaves to produce staple crops for sale to ravenous external markets, generated enormous wealth, at least for those in control of the system. For that reason, on the eve of the Civil War, the South contained some of the wealthiest counties in the United States, and in the region as a whole per capita income levels approached national levels.[2]

With the Civil War and its aftermath, however, the region suffered a catastrophic decline. The reasons for the southern economic collapse remain in dispute among historians, although most would agree that the revolutionary changes in southern agriculture resulting from Emancipation are central to the story. Whatever produced the southern economic tailspin, the results are clear: The region's per capita income was by 1880 but half that of the nation as a whole, and remained mired in that position for the next half century. Along with low incomes, as C. Vann Woodward has said, came inadequate levels of "the good things that money buys, such as education, health, protection, and the many luxuries that go to make up the celebrated American Standard of Living."[3]

Despite the omnipresence of poverty and underdevelopment in the post – Civil War South, efforts to explain that poverty, much less to do something about it, were slow to emerge. In the late nineteenth century the South was peripheral to the national consciousness, occasionally serving as a stock villain for Republican campaign oratory or as a source of quaint local color for literature and the stage. White southerners themselves, for the most part, were uncritical of their homeland. To be sure, a "New South" movement, led by journalists such as Henry W. Grady of the Atlanta *Constitution,* arose in the late nineteenth century to decry regional backwardness and to advocate industrialization and agricultural reform. However, the Gradys were less interested in analyzing the region's problems than in trumpeting its advances, and in the end buried the region's ills under an avalanche of press releases. Meanwhile, a persistent sense of grievance led most whites to identify any internal criticism with treason, and to force even the mildest dissenters into silence or exile.[4]

After 1900 there developed an increasing awareness that something was wrong with the region. Progressive-era reformers took tentative

---

[2] Robert William Fogel and Stanley L. Engerman, *Time on the Cross: The Economics of American Negro Slavery,* 2 vols. (Boston: Little, Brown, 1974), 1:247 – 57.

[3] Richard A. Easterlin, "Regional Income Trends, 1840 – 1950," in *American Economic History,* ed. Seymour E. Harris (New York: McGraw-Hill, 1961), 525 – 47, table on 528. The quote is from C. Vann Woodward, *The Burden of Southern History,* enlarged edition (Baton Rouge: Louisiana State University Press, 1968), 17.

[4] Paul M. Gaston, *The New South Creed: A Study in Southern Mythmaking* (New York: Alfred A. Knopf, 1970); Bruce Clayton, *The Savage Ideal: Intolerance and Intellectual Leadership in the South, 1890 – 1914* (Baltimore: Johns Hopkins University Press, 1972).

steps toward "uplifting" the region by modernizing its governments, expanding its social services, and mounting crusades against a variety of "social evils." However, genteel progressives showed a predilection for simplistic, moralistic solutions to southern problems, and shied away from analyses that addressed fundamental questions of power and control.[5] After World War I criticism of the South entered a more forthright, even aggressive phase. National pundits such as H. L. Mencken lampooned the cultural barrenness of the region Mencken called "the Sahara of the Bozart [Beaux Arts]"; social scientists such as Columbia University's Frank Tannenbaum catalogued the "darker phases of the South"; a new assertiveness among northern blacks, augmented in numbers and power by mass migration from the rural South to the urban North, focused attention on the injustices of lynching, segregation, and discrimination.[6]

More important, the new mood began to infuse certain white and black southerners as well. While, relative to other parts of the country, education in the South continued to be provincial and backward, progressive reformers had laid the foundations for the modern state public school systems, and a generation of academic empire-builders and philanthropists had established embryonic intellectual centers, at Vanderbilt, Fisk, North Carolina, and elsewhere. A critical mass of southerners had been exposed to intellectual currents abroad or at the modern universities of the North, such as Columbia and Chicago; returning South, they joined the burgeoning intellectual communities of the region's rising colleges and universities, forged alliances with sympathetic northern philanthropists, and inspired a younger generation in revolt against the pieties of its elders. Some of these critical observers, such as the writer William Henry Skaggs (*The Southern Oligarchy,* 1924), became expatriates; others, however, found niches in academe, in the church, in private business, in literature, and in journalism.

In the 1920s the southern intellectual community came of age and began to develop increasingly comprehensive critiques of southern life. At Vanderbilt University in Nashville, Tennessee, for instance, a literary

---

[5] William A. Link, *The Paradox of Southern Progressivism, 1880 – 1930* (Chapel Hill: University of North Carolina Press, 1992).

[6] Dewey W. Grantham, *Southern Progressivism: The Reconciliation of Progress and Tradition* (Knoxville: University of Tennessee Press, 1983); George B. Tindall, "The Benighted South: Origins of a Modern Image," in *The Ethnic Southerners* (Baton Rouge: Louisiana State University Press, 1976), 43 – 58; on the impact of the Great Migration of blacks on southern criticism, see William Cohen, "The Great Migration as a Lever for Social Change," in *Black Exodus: The Great Migration from the American South,* ed. Alferdteen Harrison (Jackson: University Press of Mississippi, 1991), 72 – 82.

group, the Fugitive poets, attracted international attention by rebelling against "the high-caste Brahmins of the Old South." In the late 1920s a core of Fugitives, in association with like-minded writers, shifted the target of their disaffection to the entire modern industrial world. In *I'll Take My Stand* (1930) the group, from then on known as the "Southern Agrarians," decried the deleterious impact of the factory, the city, commerce, and mass culture on the human spirit, and exalted the reverent, humanly scaled, close-to-the-soil society of the traditional rural South.[7]

While the Vanderbilt Agrarians were, at least initially, primarily concerned with cultural and spiritual questions, a different approach to southern problems was emerging from the other major southern intellectual center of the age, the University of North Carolina (UNC). With sociologist Howard W. Odum's creation of the journal *Social Forces* (1922) and the Institute for Research in Social Science (IRSS, 1924), the Chapel Hill institution became the foremost southern proponent of a "scientific" approach to describing and analyzing social problems; the University of North Carolina Press, headed after 1927 by W. T. Couch, disseminated the findings and ideas of southern social scientists and social critics to a broadening audience of educated southerners.[8]

More critically, the IRSS, led by Odum and including Rupert B. Vance, Guy B. Johnson, Arthur F. Raper, Thomas J. Woofter, Jr., and others, developed an intellectual framework within which the economic problems of the South could be comprehensively understood. The key concept of the group was that of the *region* — a geographically defined unit whose characteristics were interrelated, and the destinies of whose people were intertwined; thus the Odum group's approach came to be known as "Regionalism." In the eyes of the Chapel Hill Regionalists, the South (or more precisely a region they termed the "Southeast," comprising the Old Confederacy plus Kentucky but excluding Texas) was a single community whose problems were held in common, whose members were responsible for one another, and whose leaders should deal with its problems through a process of coordinated social planning. This way of thinking was by no means peculiar to the UNC group; regionalisms abounded not only in the South but elsewhere in the

[7] Paul K. Conkin, *The Southern Agrarians* (Knoxville: University of Tennessee Press, 1988).
[8] Michael O'Brien, *The Idea of the American South, 1920 – 1941* (Baltimore: Johns Hopkins University Press, 1979), 3 – 27, 213 – 27; Daniel Joseph Singal, *The War Within: From Victorian to Modernist Thought in the South, 1919 – 1945* (Chapel Hill: University of North Carolina Press, 1982), 115 – 52, 265 – 338.

America of the 1920s and 1930s. Nonetheless, Chapel Hill was the seedbed of the regionalist approach, which, along with the approach we today often call urban ecology, developed simultaneously at the University of Chicago, animated American social science for a generation. More immediately for present purposes, it was Odum's group that was primarily responsible for shaping the notion of the *South* as an appropriate unit for social enquiry, and of the problems faced by southerners as *regional* in character.[9]

The Regionalists' approach can best be seen in Odum's magnum opus, *Southern Regions of the United States* (1936; see selections below).[10] In this work Odum sought to define the region "scientifically," using a vast array of quantifiable social indexes. Significantly, the boundaries of the resulting region were determined less by culture, ethnicity, or history than by poverty and social pathology; his "Southeast" was that part of the United States most afflicted by backwardness and deprivation. Thus the Regionalists replaced the South of Confederate glory, the South of traditional culture, with a South whose very definition was "that part of the United States whose people are most deprived."

Naming, even bounding, the "southeastern" (henceforth "southern") region is not the same as explaining it; nonetheless, the Regionalists did see patterns in their lists of southern deficiencies. Thanks to the turgid prose of its author, Odum, those patterns were not readily apparent in *Southern Regions,* but the North Carolina – born Baltimore journalist Gerald W. Johnson made them accessible to a much broader audience in a book entitled *The Wasted Land* (1937).[11] As his title indicates, the central theme Johnson extracted from the welter of Odum's statistics was that of "waste": The South was a region rich in natural and human resources but had failed to use them at all efficiently. Its fertile land had been despoiled by soil exhaustion and erosion, and its people deprived of adequate education, nutrition, and health care. Moreover, the South's ablest workers were wasted by lack of opportunity and often fled the region altogether, leaving it with a disproportionate burden of the dependent young and old. Finally, the South suffered from wasted energy; a polity that should have focused on social and economic development instead dissipated its force in sterile political rhetoric and religious disputation. This

[9] O'Brien, *Idea of the American South,* 31 – 93; on regionalism more generally, see Robert L. Dorman, *Revolt of the Provinces: The Regionalist Movement in America, 1920 – 1945* (Chapel Hill: University of North Carolina Press, 1993).

[10] Howard W. Odum, *Southern Regions of the United States* (Chapel Hill: University of North Carolina Press, 1936).

[11] Gerald W. Johnson, *The Wasted Land* (Chapel Hill: University of North Carolina Press, 1937).

last point, the most politically pointed of the Regionalists' arguments, reflected Odum's and Johnson's Progressive-era view that the South's great need was for "social efficiency," and their impatience with a political and social system unamenable to "expert" control.

While the Regionalists decisively defined the region as an economic problem, and provided massive amounts of raw data for analysis, their focus on "lack of efficiency" as the problem begged an important question. As part of the United States, the American South was a society committed to capitalist, free market institutions, institutions whose major advantage was purportedly their automatic promotion of efficiency, without need for intervention by regional planners. Shouldn't "free enterprise" be solving the South's problems on its own? The Regionalists at least implied that it was not.

THE SOUTH MEETS THE NATION: THE DEPRESSION AND THE NEW DEAL

In 1929 the preoccupations of Regionalists with the failures of laissez-faire capitalism abruptly, and unexpectedly, became national preoccupations, as the United States lurched into an era of free market mechanisms gone awry. An economic slowdown beginning in that year sparked a major financial panic in October, which set in train a complex sequence of events driving the economy into a dizzying downward spiral. Banks failed, farm prices collapsed, jobs evaporated. By early 1933 over a quarter of the nonagricultural work force was unemployed, and many of the rest were on reduced wages or short time. The farm population remained "employed," but for many on the land living standards pressed the limits of subsistence, landowners lost their land, and credit was unobtainable.[12]

The calamity of the Great Depression produced a convulsion of economic soul-searching among a generation of thinkers who sought to understand why a system that had heretofore brought such prosperity seemed to be driving its erstwhile beneficiaries into poverty. At the same time, the political order so closely identified with 1920s' prosperity, dominated by the Republican party, was repudiated. The congressional elections of 1930 saw the GOP swept from power on Capitol Hill; two years later, Republican President Herbert Hoover, whose efforts to combat the Depression had proved largely ineffectual, was turned out in favor of the

[12] Lester V. Chandler, *America's Greatest Depression, 1929 – 1941* (New York: Harper & Row, 1970).

Democratic governor of New York, Franklin Delano Roosevelt, with his promise of a "New Deal" for Americans. The Roosevelt administration brought a torrent of unprecedented federal governmental activism and experimentation. Although many of the experimental programs worked at cross purposes, the New Deal era remains arguably the greatest burst of creativity in the history of American public life.[13]

Inevitably the South figured prominently in New Deal economic and social thinking. As a Democratic president, FDR depended critically on southern Democrats to support his proposals, and they in turn depended on him to provide them access to power and patronage. More important, though, the southern economy's tangled pathology now seemed a weight pulling the nation down as well. If, as many in the administration argued, the Depression was a product of "underconsumption," of an unbalanced economy in which workers produced an abundance of goods that the system denied them the wherewithal to buy, the South was far and away the most "underconsuming" part of the country.

The economic disaster had left the countryside, where most southerners still lived, in collapse; moreover, early New Deal efforts to restore the agricultural economy by raising farm prices through induced scarcity actually made matters worse for the poorest southerners. Tenants and sharecroppers, white and black, frequently found themselves deprived of benefits, of income, even of the land itself. Their plight, publicized by organizations such as the Southern Tenant Farmers' Union (STFU), attracted sympathetic attention from northern liberals and provided subject matter for some of the most powerful artistic creations of the era, notably the writings of John Steinbeck, Erskine Caldwell, and James Agee and the photography of Walker Evans, Ben Shahn, Dorothea Lange, and Margaret Bourke-White. Sympathy aside, the grinding poverty of the rural South deprived the economy of potential consumers; in an era when the ideas of economist John Maynard Keynes, stressing as they did the importance of demand to maintaining economic stability, were attracting much interest, the lack of southern "purchasing power" appeared a major impediment to recovery.[14]

[13] Arthur M. Schlesinger, Jr., *The Age of Roosevelt*, 3 vols. (Boston: Houghton Mifflin, 1957 – 60); William E. Leuchtenburg, *Franklin D. Roosevelt and the New Deal, 1932 – 1940* (New York: Harper & Row, 1963); Ellis W. Hawley, *The New Deal and the Problem of Monopoly* (Princeton, N.J.: Princeton University Press, 1966).

[14] Frank Freidel, *F.D.R. and the South* (Baton Rouge: Louisiana State University Press, 1965); Paul E. Mertz, *New Deal Policy and Southern Rural Poverty* (Baton Rouge: Louisiana State University Press, 1978); Pete Daniel, *Breaking the Land: The Transformation of Cotton, Tobacco, and Rice Cultures since 1880* (Urbana: University of Illinois Press, 1985), 65 – 236.

Moreover, the low purchasing power of the rural South pulled down that of other southerners and other Americans, notably in the manufacturing sector. In the 1920s the industrial North, long accustomed to associating Dixie with romantic plantations and rustic mountaineers, was faced with the unsettling rise of the South as a manufacturing competitor. Piedmont cotton mills, paying wages held low by a massive "reserve army" of rural poor, began to force mighty New England firms into bankruptcy, while southern chambers of commerce enticed "runaway shops," or "footloose industries," away from their old homes in New York or Philadelphia with offers of "cheap and docile" workers. The problem worsened during the Depression, which unleashed "cutthroat competition," driving wages and prices downward in a terrifying spiral. The efforts of the early New Deal to halt the process through the creation of industry cartels under the National Industrial Recovery Act of 1933 (NIRA) proved less than successful, and attracted considerable opposition from southern industrial interests who felt that northern competitors were using the federal government to nullify the South's "natural advantages." However, the experience of the NIRA piqued northern interest in using federal power to stabilize wages and working conditions; this was conspicuously true of organized labor, whose numbers were swelling and whose leaders, notably the Congress of Industrial Organizations (CIO) chieftain Sidney Hillman, were forging close political ties to the New Deal. To many nonsoutherners, the South was an enemy within, a parasitic region whose employers were benefiting from the degradation of their own labor and that of others; this sentiment ultimately led to the passage of the last major legislation of the New Deal, the Fair Labor Standards Act of 1938 (FLSA), which for the first time set federal minimum wages and maximum hours, standards that explicitly targeted southern labor practices. The FLSA, though, was only the beginning in the eyes of men such as Hillman, who saw the future of the American standard of living as dependent on solving the "problem" of the South.[15]

One other motif of New Deal economic thought, albeit not directly related to the South, had a profound impact on emerging understandings of the region's plight and its relationship to larger national concerns. The early preoccupation of the Roosevelt administration was with stabilizing an economy seemingly in free fall, and entailed a strategy of partnership between government and business. Although the early strategy succeeded in halting the downward spiral, recovery after 1933 was slow and

[15] George B. Tindall, *The Emergence of the New South, 1913 – 1945* (Baton Rouge: Louisiana State University Press, 1967), 433 – 72; Steven Fraser, *Labor Will Rule: Sidney Hillman and the Rise of American Labor* (New York: Free Press, 1991), 377 – 401.

incomplete, the national economy not regaining its 1929 vigor until the beginning of World War II. Concerns with this continuing stagnation led in several directions. Notable among these was the resurgence of an old concern with the deadening effect of finance capitalism on individual opportunity and the development of the South and West. Associated now with such legal and judicial luminaries as Supreme Court Justice Louis Brandeis and his protegé Felix Frankfurter, the new argument (actually one with deep American roots) focused on structural impediments to economic growth, impediments attributed primarily to the domination of American economic life by an oligarchy of Wall Street financiers. The antimonopoly strain of New Deal thinking found a receptive audience among southern-born administration officials, who came to Washington with a heritage of sectional and Populist suspicion of "Wall Street," and who found the antimonopoly analysis readily applicable to the problems of their home region.[16]

Moreover, the antimonopoly critique dovetailed with a theme introduced by the Regionalist Rupert Vance in his *Human Geography of the South* (1932): that the region's economy was "colonial" in character. Vance's argument was one about economic structure, not economic control: Southerners specialized in the production of low-value raw materials to be exchanged for manufactured goods produced by inhabitants of more "advanced" regions, leaving them chronically disadvantaged. The neo-Brandeisian New Dealers, though, added a political edge to Vance's diagnosis, suggesting that the region could be understood as vassal to the (northern) Money Lords — the same "economic royalists" that Franklin Roosevelt was increasingly demonizing as the great enemies of national recovery.[17]

If the enemies of the South and the enemies of Roosevelt were one and the same, the potential existed for an alliance. Moreover, the New Deal had already demonstrated its willingness to use federal spending and federal power in ways unparalleled in previous American history. Direct public works and relief spending burgeoned, providing localities with impressive infusions of outside funds, much of which went to develop what we now call "infrastructure" — roads, electric power, public buildings, civic improvements, land reclamation. The most spectacular federal involvement was the creation in 1933 of the Tennessee Valley Authority

---

[16] Hawley, *The New Deal and the Problem of Monopoly,* 281 – 379.

[17] Rupert B. Vance, *Human Geography of the South: A Study in Regional Resources and Human Adequacy* (Chapel Hill: University of North Carolina Press, 1932), 467 – 81; George B. Tindall, "The 'Colonial Economy' and the Growth Psychology: The South in the Thirties," in *Ethnic Southerners,* 209 – 23.

(TVA), conceived as a massive regionalist social laboratory. Covering all of Tennessee and portions of six other southern states, the TVA was originally conceived as a huge water power development but quickly moved to mount a comprehensive assault on the problems of the Valley, combatting malaria, reforesting cutover land, restoring worn-out fields, encouraging rural electrification, and promoting economic development in general. Although the TVA never met its more extravagant goals, it provided a model for federal involvement elsewhere, and its staff developed ideas that stimulated discourse about southern economic needs and opportunities.[18] The TVA and other New Deal activities in the region gave a growing band of southerners concerned about their region abundant reason to hope that they could draw on federal support for a more comprehensive assault on its problems.

SOUTHERN LIBERALS, THE NEW DEAL, AND THE CREATION OF THE REPORT

As we have seen, the New Deal decade was a time of ferment when increasingly acute economic problems in both the South and the nation generated a wealth of ideas about their nature and solutions. Aiding the process in the South was the creation of a loose network of southern liberals under the auspices of a group called the Southern Policy Committee (later the Southern Policy Association). The Southern Policy Committee (SPC) was the brainchild of Francis Pickens Miller. The son of a Virginia Presbyterian minister, Miller was, like many southern liberals, deeply imbued with the ethic of social-gospel Protestant Christianity, which stressed the obligation of Christians to be concerned with issues of social justice, and had previously served in a succession of posts in religion-based organizations such as the YMCA. In 1934 he joined the staff of a Washington-based liberal internationalist group, the Foreign Policy Association, and was charged with creating a network of local affiliates. Although the FPA soon abandoned the project, Miller had by then established an extensive network of contacts among educated southerners, and had shifted his attention toward domestic concerns. Accordingly, in April 1935 he asked representatives of the local groups from nine southern states to meet in Atlanta to deliberate on southern policy

---

[18] On TVA, Tindall, *Emergence of the New South*, 446 – 57; Richard Lowitt, "The TVA, 1933 – 1945," in *TVA: Fifty Years of Grass-Roots Bureaucracy*, ed. Erwin C. Hargrove and Paul K. Conkin (Urbana: University of Illinois Press, 1983), 35 – 65.

questions, a meeting that resulted in the creation of the Southern Policy Committee.[19]

Miller's intent in establishing the SPC was shaped by an old Progressive notion, that reasonable people of goodwill could determine a "common good" above the contentions of private interests, but that their voices were lost in the din of partisanship and special pleading. He thus envisioned the Southern Policy Committee as a sort of "people's lobby" (an intent not unlike that of the modern-day Common Cause). In this quest he was less than successful. Early gatherings of the SPC strove for inclusiveness, but got bogged down in contentions between Regionalists and their major southern intellectual rivals, the Nashville-based Southern Agrarians, who had by this time moved beyond their cultural critique of "industrialism" to advance a radical "back-to-the-land" agenda. Hopelessly outnumbered, the Agrarians soon withdrew from active participation, leaving the organization dominated by Regionalists and liberals of a New Deal bent, including the renegade Agrarian Herman Clarence Nixon. Socially it remained narrowly based. While it made tentative steps to include blacks (notably sociologist and Fisk University President Charles S. Johnson), its white, overwhelmingly male, membership was largely based in the academy and in social-service institutions; few businessmen or working people belonged. One major exception to the rule was the involvement of a number of journalists, notably Barry Bingham and Mark Ethridge of the Louisville *Courier-Journal*, Jonathan Daniels of the Raleigh *News and Observer*, Virginius Dabney of the Richmond *Times-Dispatch*, George Fort Milton of the Chattanooga *News*, Clarence Poe of the *Progressive Farmer*, the leading southern farm journal, and columnist John Temple Graves II of Birmingham. By providing these few, but articulate, white liberal southerners with a place to meet and exchange ideas, the SPC was a major incubator for the emerging synthesis ultimately embodied in the *Report on Economic Conditions of the South*.

Apart from its periodic conferences and its publication of a series of *Southern Policy Papers* through the University of North Carolina Press, the SPC was a decentralized group whose local affiliates were frequently as important as the parent. The Alabama Policy Committee, for instance, published its own papers and nurtured a populist sensibility all its own.

[19] On the coalescence of New Deal – era southern liberalism, see Bruce J. Schulman, *From Cotton Belt to Sunbelt: Federal Policy, Economic Development, and the Transformation of the South, 1938 – 1980* (New York: Oxford University Press, 1991), 39 – 44. On Miller and the SPC, see Francis Pickens Miller, *Man from the Valley: Memoirs of a 20th-Century Virginian* (Chapel Hill: University of North Carolina Press, 1971), esp. 78 – 84.

Even more important, though, was the Washington affiliate, which brought together liberal laypeople, southern Roosevelt administration officials, and pro-FDR southern politicians in periodic meetings at Hall's Restaurant; hence it was sometimes called the "Hall's Restaurant group." Francis Miller and Brooks Hays, an Arkansan then serving in the Resettlement Administration, a New Deal agency devoted to providing land for unemployed and dispossessed people, convened the group, although Alabama Congressman Lister Hill apparently played an important organizing role as well; other politicians involved included John Sparkman, W. R. Poage, and, occasionally, a young congressional aide named Lyndon B. Johnson.[20]

Another regular at the Hall's meetings was a young Georgian named Clark Foreman. Foreman was born in Atlanta in 1902 to a prominent family; his mother's brother was Clark Howell, the publisher of the Atlanta *Constitution*. After an education that included studies at Harvard and the London School of Economics, Foreman, who had early developed a concern with race issues, joined the staff of the Commission on Interracial Cooperation, the principal southern race relations organization of the 1920s and 1930s. He soon moved north to engage in philanthropic work, notably for the Julius Rosenwald Fund, a foundation created by Rosenwald, a Chicago merchant prince (Sears, Roebuck and Company), to support black education. In 1933 he joined Secretary Harold L. Ickes's Interior Department as the New Deal's conduit to the black community, later moving on to head the Power Division of the Public Works Administration. At some point in 1937 or early 1938, Foreman recalled ten years later, he was attending one of the Hall's gatherings along with a guest, Power Division Counsel Jerome Frank. Frank, one of the leading mentors of the left New Dealers, suggested that the group present its views to the public. Foreman mentally filed the suggestion away, until soon afterward he received a fateful summons to meet with the president.[21]

In the spring of 1938 Franklin Roosevelt had special reasons to be worried about the South. Despite his landslide reelection victory just a year and a half earlier, his leadership was in serious trouble. He had been defeated in his 1937 assault on the Supreme Court, the nation's major

[20] Conkin, *The Southern Agrarians,* 114–18; Donald Davidson, "Where Are the Laymen? A Study in Policy-Making" *American Review* 9 (November 1937): 456–81; Sara N. Shouse, *Hillbilly Realist: Herman Clarence Nixon of Possum Trot* (Tuscaloosa: University of Alabama Press, 1986), 78–94; Schulman, *From Cotton Belt to Sunbelt,* 42–43.

[21] On Foreman's early career, see Interview with Clark Foreman, by Jacquelyn Hall and Bill Finger, November 1974, Southern Oral History Program Collection, Southern Historical Collection, the Library of the University of North Carolina at Chapel Hill, 1–39.

industries were embroiled in labor strife, and the New Deal's principal political asset, the economic recovery that had begun in 1933, had gone into reverse. More seriously, FDR was facing increasingly open revolt within his own Democratic party ranks, notably in its southern flank. While most southern politicians had endorsed the early New Deal, many remained wary of the federal intrusion it involved, and even warier of what they feared were "radical" influences within the administration. That wariness was by late 1937 turning to open disaffection, with conservative Democrats such as Virginia's Carter Glass and Harry F. Byrd, North Carolina's Josiah W. Bailey, South Carolina's Ellison D. ("Cotton Ed") Smith, and Georgia's Walter F. George openly cooperating with the Republican minority to block administration initiatives.[22]

Roosevelt himself, though, remained enormously popular, not only with the American people in general but with southerners in particular, as was indicated by a newly developed device, the national opinion poll. Furthermore, in early 1938 the president had reason to believe that his popularity might be transferable; spring senatorial primaries in two southern states, Florida and Alabama, saw smashing victories for Claude Pepper and Lister Hill, both ardent New Dealers and proponents of the Fair Labor Standards Act, a Roosevelt initiative fiercely opposed by southern conservative Democrats. Those factors led FDR to believe that he could make use of his personal appeal with southerners to topple his southern conservative enemies within the party.

A prominent target of his planned "purge" was Georgia Senator Walter George — but plotting strategy against George required that he consult with those knowledgeable about politics in that state, and it was for that reason that he had invited Foreman into the Oval Office. Having been away from his home state for some years, Foreman could offer no advice on the local scene; however, he did have one suggestion, drawn from his earlier discussions with Frank: that the administration prepare a pamphlet detailing the benefits of the New Deal to the South. Roosevelt was instantly taken by the idea, but suggested one important modification: that the pamphlet not deal with the New Deal or with any proposed solution to southern problems, but merely set forth the facts of the South's economic plight. According to Foreman's 1948 recollection, Roosevelt felt that "if the people understand the facts . . . they will find their own remedies"; more likely he was concerned with

[22] The standard discussion is James T. Patterson, *Congressional Conservatism and the New Deal: The Growth of the Conservative Coalition in Congress, 1933 – 1939* (Lexington: University of Kentucky Press, 1967); see also Dewey W. Grantham, *The Life and Death of the Solid South: A Political History* (Lexington: University Press of Kentucky, 1988), 108 – 12.

maintaining his own flexibility. Nonetheless, Foreman took his suggestion to heart; the final *Report* was notable for its lack of recommendations for action.[23]

Roosevelt also suggested that Foreman take the idea to Lowell Mellett, executive director of the National Emergency Council. The NEC originated as a coordinating body for the special recovery agencies of the early New Deal. After 1935, though, the agency declined in importance, being characterized by one commentator as "a somnolent organ that gathered information, answered questions, and clipped newspapers." It gained a new lease on life, and a sharp change of direction, with the appointment in 1937 of Lowell Mellett as executive director. Mellett had been a crusading editor with the Scripps-Howard newspaper chain until he fell out with top management over his advocacy of Roosevelt's attempt to remake the Supreme Court. Out of appreciation for the newsman's past support, the president appointed him to head the NEC. Mellett quickly turned the agency into a major public relations operation for the administration, providing research and publicity services to congressmen, the media, and, through government-produced motion pictures, the general public. Through an extensive network of state councils he provided the president with channels of communication independent of the media and the federal bureaucracy.[24]

Mellett was at first timid about Foreman's proposal; however, he subsequently changed his mind and agreed to take it under his wing, offering the extensive information-gathering capacity of his agency in assistance. The plan was to produce a pamphlet of roughly sixty to eighty pages, divided into four-page topical sections that could be readily detached and distributed separately. The actual writing was done during June 1938 by Foreman and an ad hoc group of southern New Dealers drawn from the Hall's Restaurant group and Foreman's circle of acquaintances. Chief among Foreman's associates were Arthur ("Tex") Goldschmidt, Foreman's assistant at the PWA Power Division; Jack Fischer, another Texan who was information director of the Farm Security Administration; and Alabamian Clifford Durr, counsel to the Reconstruction Finance Corporation. Other southerners from New Deal agencies such

[23] The basic account of the origins of the *Report* is Clark Foreman to Gay Morenus, November 24, 1948, in Southern Conference for Human Welfare Papers, Division of Archives/Special Collections, Woodruff Library, Atlanta University Center, Collection 19, Box 41 (hereafter SCHW Papers). Other general accounts of the history of the *Report* include Steve Davis, " The South as ' The Nation's No. 1 Economic Problem': The NEC Report of 1938" *Georgia Historical Quarterly* 62 (Summer 1978): 119 – 32; and Mertz, *New Deal Policy and Southern Rural Poverty*, 221 – 52.

[24] On Mellett, see *Current Biography, 1942* (New York: H. W. Wilson, 1942), 583 – 85.

as the Works Progress Administration, the TVA, the Securities and Exchange Commission (SEC), and the Department of Labor made important contributions.[25]

The initial product of their labors comprised seventeen brief sections. In contrast to the final version, the preliminary draft offered not simply a description of southern economic woes, but a sometimes sharply worded diagnosis of them. The "wasted land" arguments of Odum and Johnson got considerable play, but the informing principle of the draft was the antimonopoly version of the argument that the South was a "colonial economy." Time and again the authors blamed the ills of the South on the region's "colonial" status. Southern dependence on outside development capital had resulted in a chronic drain of profits to Wall Street. Nonsouthern ownership of natural resources had stifled their development. "Carpetbaggers" of industry had invaded the region in search of readily exploitable labor and subsidies from localities desperate for payrolls, aided by early state industrial development schemes such as Mississippi's Balance Agriculture with Industry (BAWI) program. Finally, northern manufacturers had used their historic political hegemony to shape federal policies that discriminated against the South. Northerners' control of railroads and of federal regulation had allowed them to force southern shippers to pay higher rates than shippers in other parts of the country. Their dominance of Congress had permitted them to levy high protective tariffs on manufactured imports, a practice that indirectly subsidized northern industry while both raising prices to southern consumers and damaging the export markets for southern farm products. Ultimately to blame for these impediments was the ascendence of Wall Street in American business life; in its most polemical language, the draft declared that

> the South, which is one of our wealthiest sections, is at the same time the poorest. It is wealthy in natural resources and advantages and poor in ownership and control of the money and credit resources necessary for their development and exchange. As a result it must sit by and watch its plenty enjoyed by other sections not so abundantly blessed by nature but in control of the man-made machinery of finance. It is the victim of a fiction — that money and credit, the machinery created for the more effective distribution of wealth, is wealth itself — a fiction which by general acceptance has become more powerful than truth and has forced the South to dissipate its capital in order to exist; to deliver its material resources into the hands of

[25] Foreman to Morenus; Lucia M. Pitts (Secretary to Clark Foreman) to "Miss Foster," NEC, August 4, 1938, SCHW Papers.

others without consideration except an inadequate wage for the labor of removing them from the ground.[26]

The draft's hostility to outside investment in the South raised an obvious objection; that the *absence* of such investment would place the region in an even worse situation. The draft, then, coupled its diagnosis of the southern malady with a prescription for economic development that avoided dependence on imported capital. In a section entitled "New Industries," the writers suggested that the region make innovative use of its natural and agricultural resources to develop "sound native industries; it has no need to lure 'run-away' industries from other regions through offering such inducements as subsidies and cheap labor." Here the writers were drawing in part upon the emerging "chemurgy" movement, which sought to use sophisticated chemistry to find new industrial uses for farm and forest products. Chemurgy was fashionable in the interwar South; scientists such as Charles H. Herty and the black Tuskegee chemist George Washington Carver were famous for their wizardry with the humblest of southern plants, the pine tree, the peanut, and the sweet potato.[27]

More broadly, the draft echoed a broader concern of Depression-era America — that a harsh imbalance had arisen between urban-industrial and rural America that was economically and spiritually poisoning both. While some groups, such as the Vanderbilt Agrarians, called for a return to the land, many others, both within and outside the South, sought a synthesis between agricultural and industrial life, calling for decentralized manufacturing closely tied to local rural productions, frequently organized as cooperative enterprises. This organic vision, of a close-knit, economically interdependent community of human scale, was prominent in *Southern Regions* and in the approach of the early TVA; it gained expression in communitarian experiments underwritten both by private reformers and New Deal agencies such as the Resettlement Administration and the Farm Security Administration; and gained political expression in the pronouncements of Arkansas Governor Carl E. Bailey. Finally, an emphasis on "home-grown" industry fit well with the concerns of labor allies of the New Deal, such as Sidney Hillman of the CIO's Amalgamated Clothing Workers, that the South needed to be cured of its eagerness to attract "runaway" shops with the lure of cheap labor, a practice that not

[26] A copy of the preliminary draft is in the SCHW Papers. The quote is from the concluding paragraph of preliminary Section 1, "Economic Resources."

[27] The manifesto of the "chemurgy" movement is William J. Hale, *The Farm Chemurgic: Farmward the Star of Destiny Lights Our Way* (Boston: Stratford Company, 1934). On the "chemurgy" movement and the South, see Tindall, *Emergence of the New South*, 465 – 66.

only reinforced southern poverty but undercut northern workers (and their unions) as well.[28]

Clearly, despite the president's request that it be confined to "facts," the draft *Report* had something of a programmatic vision of southern development; it likewise went beyond its mandate by promoting federal government involvement in providing solutions. Several passages in the preliminary version spoke positively of federal public works projects, notably in flood control. Accusations that the wage differential between southern and northern workers helped perpetuate the region's economic disadvantage read like a brief for the Fair Labor Standards Act, which gained congressional passage while the draft was in process. One entire section treated "Unemployment and Relief "; its author credited the advent of federal relief in 1933 for bringing "graphically before the public evidence of the widespread poverty which had previously, for the most part, been either accepted or ignored." While arguing that relief monies expended thus far had been hopelessly inadequate to the task of alleviating southern poverty, the author contended that the machinery of relief, combined with the use of the federal income tax, could prove a major means by which wealth could be redistributed southward to provide much-needed "purchasing power" to the mass of southerners. Thus, notwithstanding their charge to be purely descriptive of southern problems, the authors of the report clearly had another purpose in mind as well: advocacy of an unprecedented program of federal aid to poor southerners, justified as a form of "reparation" for past injustices.

Concerned that the pamphlet not be seen purely as administration propaganda, Mellett and Foreman decided to present their preliminary draft to "a sort of sponsoring committee" of well-known southerners. However, they evidently gave less care to the composition of the Advisory Committee than to the writing itself. Their initial choice as chair, Howard Odum, was contacted in late June, less than two weeks before the planned meeting date of July 5; Odum declined, partly because of prior commitments, partly out of fear that his reputation as an unbiased scientist might be tarnished by association with what he regarded as a New Deal enterprise. Foreman and Mellett then turned to Odum's colleague, UNC President Frank Porter Graham. Graham was by 1938 well-established as the embodiment of southern liberalism, a social-gospel Christian

---

[28] Mertz, *New Deal Policy and Southern Rural Poverty,* esp. 166 – 78; Paul K. Conkin, *Tomorrow a New World: The New Deal Community Program* (Ithaca, N.Y.: Cornell University Press, 1959); Edward J. Meeman, "The South and Industry: Discussion by the National Policy Committee at Memphis, October 16, 1937" (pamphlet in Herman Clarence Nixon Papers, Special Collections, Vanderbilt University Library), 5; Fraser, *Labor Will Rule,* 384 – 86.

involved in a plethora of causes; he readily accepted the summons from Washington. The remaining twenty-one members of the committee were well balanced by state and by occupation; while academics were over-represented, with six members, the group also included two manufacturers, a banker, an airline executive, a power company official, two agricultural spokesmen, and three lawyers. Barry Bingham was one of two journalists on the panel, and Governor Carl E. Bailey of Arkansas was one of two government officials. Southern labor was represented by three union leaders, notably H. L. Mitchell of the Southern Tenant Farmers' Union, and Lucy Randolph Mason of the Congress of Industrial Organizations.[29]

At their meeting July 5, the Advisory Committee was presented with mimeographed copies of each of the seventeen original sections, which Foreman systematically read through, inviting comments and suggestions. According to Foreman's recollection, the committee accepted the draft with few changes, though subsequent revisions (discussed below) suggest that conferees raised significant concerns about the *Report*'s emphases. One participant, Mitchell, brought a formal statement from the STFU calling for a vastly expanded program to resettle displaced farmworkers on subsistence homesteads; no other conferee seems to have come with a well-developed agenda. One other item of business was the reading by Mellett of a letter from Roosevelt endorsing the project. This letter, drafted by Mellett for the president's signature, became the basic thematic statement of the *Report.* In the letter FDR attributed his concern for the South to his longstanding part-time residence in Georgia and his close ties to many southerners. More important, though, he stressed the significance of aiding the South to restoring America's national economic health.

> It is my conviction that the South presents right now the Nation's No. 1 economic problem — the Nation's problem, not merely the South's. For we have an economic unbalance in the Nation as a whole, due to this very condition of the South.
> It is an unbalance that can and must be righted, for the sake of the South and of the Nation.

Inadvertently, these ringing phrases became instantly notorious. A reporter for the *New York Times* slipped into the meeting room while the

[29] On the Advisory Committee, see Clark Foreman Interview, 42. On Odum's attitude, see Howard W. Odum to Clark Foreman, June 24, 1938, SCHW Papers; Odum to Gerald W. Johnson, July 16, 1938, Howard Washington Odum Papers, Southern Historical Collection, the Library of the University of North Carolina at Chapel Hill (hereafter Odum Papers), 1938, folder 443. On Graham, see Warren Ashby, *Frank Porter Graham: A Southern Liberal* (Winston-Salem, N.C.: John F. Blair, 1980).

conferees were at lunch, pilfering a copy of the preliminary draft with cover letter. The following day, "South Is Declared 'No. 1' by President in Economic Need" was the banner headline in the *Times*, and the ensuing article led with FDR's characterization of the South as a "drag on the Nation" and a source of "imbalance" requiring an "imperative" end. The entire text of the president's letter was included, along with brief summaries of the first five preliminary sections.[30]

The leak, partial and premature as it was, was unfortunate, for the *Report* quickly became a lightning rod for controversy. Northern conservative outlets such as the *Times* sniffed at its hostility to outside ownership of southern resources and industry. Saying that "this seems to be merely a sinister way of saying that Northern capital has flowed into the South," the *Times*'s editorialist noted that industrial America had been built in large part with an influx of British investment, and contended that the South was benefiting in similar fashion from outside investment. The bulk of the negative response, though, poured forth from the South itself. "New South" boosters, who regarded negative publicity as bad for business, reacted to the open discussion of regional problems with howls of wounded pride and denial; one North Carolina paper charged that the *Report* and its intellectual inspirers, Odum and Johnson, were "reduc[ing] State and regional advertising to a pitiful and expensive deception." Southern conservatives, for their part, immediately feared the political implications of the *Report;* it was generally expected that the final version would include recommendations for federal action, and that these would entail massive federal intervention in southern economic and social life. Senator Josiah Bailey of North Carolina harrumphed that the South was handling its own problems perfectly well; while "there is too much poverty in the South, . . . we will not get rid of it by giving people money." Senator John E. Miller of Arkansas contended that what the region most needed was to be let alone. North Carolinian David Clark, a sharp-tongued spokesman for the southern textile industry, declared the Advisory Committee a "slumming commission," and particularly scored the participation of CIO official Lucy Mason and of Graham, a long-time bête noire of the industry for his advocacy of workers' concerns (a Clark editorial appears on p. 135).[31]

[30] The account of the meeting is drawn from Foreman Interview, 42; Foreman to Morenus, SCHW Papers; Mertz, *New Deal Policy and Southern Rural Poverty,* 234; *New York Times,* July 6, 1938, 1.
[31] Editorial, "No. 1 Economic Problem," *New York Times,* July 7, 1938, p. 18; ed., "Flapdoodle," *High Point [N.C.] Enterprise,* July 6, 1938, clipping encl. in Henry Foscue to Frank P. Graham, July 19, 1938, Frank P. Graham Papers, Southern Historical Collection, The Library of the University of North Carolina at Chapel Hill (hereafter Graham Papers), Series 1.1, 1938, folder 66; *New York Times,* July 10, August 13, 1938, "Roosevelt Appoints a Slumming Commission," *Textile Bulletin,* July 7, 1938.

While controversy stirred, revision of the *Report* proceeded. The preliminary draft, the product of many hands, required a great deal of reorganization and tightening; facts and figures were rechecked for accuracy, and suggestions of the committee and interested outsiders were incorporated. The language of the *Report* also shifted in tone. While "economic colonialism" remained a central theme, allegations of absentee ownership were tempered with the realization that much southern industry, notably cotton textiles, was in fact of indigenous origin, and the sweeping attack on finance capital at the end of the first section was eliminated. Programmatic passages were systematically purged, particularly those advocating decentralized, rural-based industry and specific federal policies; thus the entire section on "Unemployment and Relief" was axed. The revised *Report* was thus considerably less belligerent and sectional than earlier. On the other hand, changes were made bringing the *Report* into closer harmony with FDR's theme: that aiding the South would be a positive good to the nation as well. A new conclusion to the "Population" section, for instance, stressed that "the population problems of the South . . . are not local problems alone. . . . these problems are national." Echoing Frank Graham's personal interest in federal aid to education, the introduction to the "Education" section built on the point to note that heavy migration out of the South "makes poor schooling in any region a matter of national concern." Most important, the revised *Report* included an entire new section, "Purchasing Power," which built on the "underconsumption" analysis of the Depression to argue that an attack on southern poverty would, by creating vast new markets for manufactured goods, aid in putting Americans throughout the nation back to work.[32]

RELEASE AND RECEPTION

By August 6 the *Report* was ready; the NEC printed 100,000 copies, with copies of individual sections printed as leaflets. In offering it to the president, Mellett declared that "the effort has been made to have it unimpeachable as to facts, while simple enough to be understood by any reader," goals he felt had largely been achieved.[33] Roosevelt, in the meantime, had purposes of his own. In late June he had announced his

[32] On revision, see Frank P. Graham to Carl E. Bailey, July 22, 1938; Graham to Stuart Rabb, July 28, 1938, Graham Papers, Series 1.1, 1938, folder 66.

[33] Lowell Mellett to Franklin Roosevelt, August 6, 1938, Franklin Delano Roosevelt Papers, Official File 788, Franklin D. Roosevelt Library, Hyde Park, N.Y.

intent to intervene against conservative opponents in Democratic party primaries, and had in early July departed Washington on a circuitous train trip across the country, embracing and snubbing as he went. In California he had boarded a ship for a cruise through the Panama Canal; by August 9, when he landed in Pensacola, Florida, to begin the southeastern leg of his tour, the *Report* was awaiting him and scheduled for release August 10. On the day of the release, while resting in Warm Springs, Georgia, FDR announced his endorsement of Lawrence Camp, an otherwise obscure opponent of his principal purge target, Senator Walter George of Georgia.[34]

The following day, sitting with George and Camp on the platform at the dedication of a rural electrification project in Barnesville, Georgia, Roosevelt formally introduced the *Report* to the public (the complete text of the Barnesville speech is reprinted starting on p. 129). Significantly, he did so with open political intent. The problems revealed in the *Report's* fifteen sections were so varied that no single solution, no panacea, would do; "the battlefront," he declared, "extends over thousands of miles and we must push forward along the whole front at the same time." Moreover, the South's traditional predilection for "states' rights" would not suffice; a federal campaign was required, one led by a president of national vision and proven sympathy for the region. For such a long-term, broad-front campaign, Roosevelt would need congressional supporters of consistent loyalty and good faith. Roosevelt then dropped the bombshell for which the Barnesville address became famous; in George's presence he declared of his fellow Democrat that "on most public questions he and I do not speak the same language."[35]

Insofar as Roosevelt had intended to use the "purge" to mobilize southerners behind the *Report* (and not vice versa), the result of the Barnesville speech was to entangle the *Report* hopelessly in what soon became one of the greatest political disasters of his administration. The president's intervention into what many white southern voters regarded as their own affairs backfired; by late August columnist John Temple Graves II was declaring that "The President has called the South a No. 1 economic problem and he has made it a No. 1 political problem." George won renomination handily, with Camp polling a pathetic third; another of FDR's southern targets, Senator Ellison D. ("Cotton Ed") Smith of South Carolina, likewise won his primary with ease. Roosevelt's enormous

---

[34] On Roosevelt's "purge" tour, see James McGregor Burns, *Roosevelt: The Lion and the Fox* (New York: Harcourt, Brace and World, 1956), 361 – 63.

[35] *The Public Papers and Addresses of Franklin D. Roosevelt, 1938 Volume* (New York: Macmillan, 1941), 463 – 70.

personal popularity notwithstanding, southern primary voters resented outside interference, and local issues and alignments generally counted more heavily than a president's preferences. Some liberals saw a more sinister significance to the results in the fact that the most ardent southern supporters of the New Deal, blacks and poor whites, were largely disfranchised; indeed, the failure of the purge proved an impetus to liberal attacks on the panoply of restrictive voting laws that helped undergird the region's rigid political structure. The *Report*'s political use by the president reinforced the conclusion of all too many people that the document was, despite its neutral veneer, a New Deal tract — a belief that impeded its reception and gave vested interests license to launch unreasonable attacks upon it.[36]

Despite its messy political associations, the *Report*'s final appearance met with strikingly broad favor. Unfiltered through fragmentary news accounts and critical glosses, its stylistic simplicity, careful avoidance of polemic, and straightforward presentation of data proved appealing to large numbers of educated southerners. Since the *Report* was in large part a synthesis of work that had gone on for many years and had reached broad audiences through southern newspapers and the University of North Carolina Press, commentators rightly noted that, for all the initial hue and cry, it contained few surprises to those familiar with the region. The *Report*'s most politically pointed passages, its denunciations of northern discrimination against southern commerce and industry, struck a chord among even more conservative southerners long accustomed to expressions of sectional grievance; the Atlanta *Constitution* hoped that it would force the rest of the country to realize that "the South has been oppressed for 75 years by an industrial east and middle west for selfish ends."[37]

By one measure — public interest — the *Report* was an enormous success. From the outset demand for the *Report* was huge, and possibly half a million copies were distributed by the end of 1938. Many of these were distributed en masse by civic groups and schools, which saw the pamphlet as a cheap, accessible primer on southern problems. Public and private agencies in Georgia and South Carolina issued their own editions of the *Report*, with annotations comparing its findings to conditions in their respective states. Frank Graham found it being studied "way back

[36] On the failure of the "purge," see Tindall, *Emergence of the New South*, 627 – 30; Basil Rauch, *The History of the New Deal* (New York: Capricorn Books, 1963), 318 – 19; Davis, "South as 'the Nation's No. 1 Economic Problem,'" 125 – 26, 129.

[37] On response to the *Report*, see Davis, "South as 'the Nation's No. 1 Economic Problem,'" 123 – 25, 127; ed., "Facing the Facts," Winston-Salem *Journal*, August 14, 1938.

in the mountains of North Carolina without prejudice and without resentment."[38]

While the appearance of the *Report* thus attracted much favorable attention, it also gave its intraregional critics a target; within a short time they began their own counterattack. Most criticism, to be sure, was weakened by its misrepresentation of the *Report*'s objectives. Its southern detractors generally proceeded from the assumption of civic boosters that any adverse publicity had to be motivated by northern desires to "run down" their southern competitors. Thus southern promotional organs such as the *Manufacturers' Record* of Baltimore, ignoring the southern authorship of the document, insisted that its purpose was "to arraign the South . . . as the sore spot of the country." Why? "The *progress* the South is making," it continued, "is of grave concern to other sections which do not want southern freight rates equalized with theirs," implying a sectional animus to the *Report* that was patently absurd. The *Manufacturers' Record,* and such other influential critics as Fitzgerald Hall of the Nashville-based Southern States Industrial Council (SSIC), responded with their own cannonade of figures (Hall's critique, with a response from Lowell Mellett, appears on p. 139). However, they were generally less concerned with constructing a coherent statistical case of their own than with picking petty quarrels over minor details; given the dependence of statistics on the context in which they are gathered and used, it proved easy to deploy figures that seemed to contradict those in the *Report.*[39]

The disingenuousness of such criticism stemmed from a half-hidden agenda, for the *Report* contained implicit threats to numerous vested interests in the South, threats amplified by the close association of the *Report* with FDR's attempted purge of conservatives. Rumors swept the southern textile industry that the federal government was preparing to build its own cotton mills; just as the creation of the TVA was justified as providing a "yardstick" by which to judge the "fairness" of private power rates, so these would be used to test traditional southern industrialists' justifications for their historically low wage rates. Even the *Report*'s broadly popular attack on railroad freight rate differentials gored some

---

[38] Frank P. Graham to Gilbert T. Stephenson, November 30, 1938, Graham Papers, Series 1.1, 1938, folder 73; Mertz, *New Deal Policy and Southern Rural Poverty,* 240.

[39] Editorial, "The Facts' of the Economic Report," *Manufacturers' Record* 107 (September 1938): 21 – 23; "More Facts about the South," *Manufacturers' Record* 107 (November 1938): 19 – 21; Fitzgerald Hall, "Comments on the Report of [sic] Economic Conditions of the South," September 7, 1938; copy in the Graham Papers, Series 1.1, 1938, folder 70. The response of the writers of the *Report* is enclosed in Lowell Mellett to Fitzgerald Hall, September 19, 1938, in Graham Papers, Series 1.1, 1938, folder 70. Both Hall's comment and Mellett's response were made public.

southern industrial oxen, notably those represented by Hall and the SSIC, producers of low-value commodities who had long since cut favorable deals with the railroads and were fearful of losing them.[40]

While much of this criticism was specious, though, one charge was revealing, both of the climate of the South at that time and of a central weakness of the *Report* itself. It was common for critics to contend that a document couching the problem of southern poverty in *regional* terms was unfair — to *whites*. One major difference between the South and other parts of the United States, Hall argued, was "the fact that 29 per cent of its population is colored. . . . the standard of living and the income of Negroes everywhere in the United States, in general, is lower than that of the white population." The South suffered peculiarly, claimed Josiah Bailey in a letter to Frank Graham, from the presence of "2½ millions of negro workers, many of whom are not disposed to work constantly, very few of whom are disposed to try to accumulate." White detractors of the *Report* complained that, by lumping blacks and whites into a single "problem," it badly downplayed the economic prosperity of whites.[41]

By thus raising the race issue, critics of the *Report* were attacking its fundamental presumption: that the problem of poverty *in the South* was a problem of *southern poverty*, rooted not in individuals or races but in the region itself. To its critics, on the other hand, poverty was a product of personal (or racial) deficiency, with no relationship to the social context in which white and black southerners lived. Southern poverty, to them, was a statistical accident, the product of an abnormal concentration of "inferior" people in the region. Their assumption was rejected outright by the creators of the *Report;* Mellett, Foreman, and their associates insisted, first, that the heavily black character of southern poverty did not excuse its existence, and, second, that in any case "the Negro has no monopoly on poverty in the South."[42] In their pursuit of what was essentially a "divide-and-conquer" strategy, white supremacist critics sought to deny what to a generation of southern social analysts was the obvious: that the economic disabilities of southerners, black and white, were a function of their membership in a disadvantaged community.

Nonetheless, racist criticism pointed up a major flaw in the *Report:* its own neglect of the racial dimension of southern problems. While it makes

[40] *New York Times*, August 13, 1938, p. 1; William H. Joubert, *Southern Freight Rates in Transition* (Gainesville: University of Florida Press, 1949), 368 – 70.

[41] Hall, "Comment on Report," 1 – 2; Josiah Bailey to Frank P. Graham, April 12, 1939, Graham Papers, Series 1.1, 1939, folder 57; see also remarks of Bailey in debate with Graham on the Town Hall of the Air, Chapel Hill, N.C., March 30, 1939, *Congressional Record*, Vol. 84, Part 14, 76th Congress, First Session, 3904.

[42] Mellett to Hall, September 19, 1938, 3.

occasional passing reference to special problems faced by blacks in the areas of employment, health, and general living standards, it overwhelmingly prefers to lump whites and blacks together. One striking example is the section on education: Its catalogue of southern school problems not only ignores blacks, it completely omits any discussion of segregation, even to mention a by-then standard argument, that the "necessity" of financing a dual school system imposed extra costs on an already poor region. That the authors failed squarely to confront the race issue owed something to their own racial attitudes. Even though Foreman and Graham had longstanding ties to the black civil rights community, were opposed to the more egregious disfranchisement laws, and would become leading advocates of racial equality after World War II, they were not yet ready to challenge the principle of "separate but equal" — and most southern liberals were less advanced than they.[43] Liberals' moderation had much to do with the logic of regionalism, which was less concerned with racial justice than with the elevation of the region's people without regard to race. There were political reasons as well for their attitude; the federal programs they advocated had little chance of enactment if southern whites allowed their fears of a new Reconstruction to obscure their need of outside help. Whites had to be taught that their interests as southerners were more important than their interests as whites. But what if that lesson weren't learned? The consequences, as southern liberals were ruefully to discover, would be damaging.[44]

THE FAILURE TO FOLLOW UP

While the creators of the *Report* were contending with its critics, its sympathizers were asking a different question: What was to be done? Even during the *Report*'s preparation, some members of the Advisory Committee were concerned that it lacked a positive program. J. Skottowe Wannamaker, head of a cotton cooperative based in South Carolina, believed that the Committee should be reconvened to make policy recommendations and feared that failure to do so would allow the *Report*'s detractors to dismiss it as a political dodge. Mounting calls for a new meeting of the Committee, though, met with silence from Washington. Mellett indicated privately that the administration preferred that south-

---

[43] On this matter see Morton Sosna, *In Search of the Silent South: Southern Liberals and the Race Issue* (New York: Columbia University Press, 1977).

[44] A more sinister explanation of the *Report*'s neglect of race is offered in Basil Rauch, *History of the New Deal*, 322 – 23.

erners develop their own program, one that would not be seen as an imposition by the New Deal. However, given the clear call in the *Report* for *federal* action, and the unlikelihood that nonsouthern support could be mobilized around proposals of southern sectional origin, this explanation seems incomplete. More likely, Roosevelt's interest in the *Report* had faded along with its immediate political usefulness. By the end of August it was evident that the purge had failed, and with its failure went the best hope for continuing the New Deal in any effective form. Furthermore, in late 1938 FDR was anticipating the greatest battle of his life, against the totalitarians abroad and the isolationists at home. On the other hand, the *Report* remained useful as a rallying cry for New Deal adherents in the South and a tool for mobilizing them against his regional opponents; the president would, accordingly, lend them sympathetic support through such surrogates as his wife Eleanor, but would not risk valuable political capital through active support of a legislative program. If the *Report* was to have an impact on the nation, the response to it would have to come from quarters outside the administration.[45]

The major followup to the *Report*, then, would not be a slate of New Deal legislative proposals, but the encouragement of an insurgent movement within the region. Its vehicle was a conclave, the Southern Conference for Human Welfare (SCHW), called by a group of Alabamians loosely associated with the Alabama Policy Committee to meet in Birmingham that November. Billed as the South's response to the NEC *Report*, the Conference attracted over 1,200 delegates, the greatest gathering of southern liberals to that time in the region's history. New Dealers were prominent in the gathering; Eleanor Roosevelt and Hugo Black were the most eminent, and Foreman became a leader of the organization created at the meeting. The delegates divided into numerous task forces to devise proposals on a vast array of problems; these were submitted to a Resolutions Committee, which combined them into thirty-seven groups for endorsement by the full assembly (the text of the resolutions appears on pp. 149 – 60).

While the SCHW convened in an atmosphere of great expectation, its response to the *Report* had no effect on events. Its failure was due in part to the diffuse character of its membership and concerns. As an effort to create a "united front," it included leading radicals, even some members of the Communist party, whose presence was used by conservatives to

[45] J. Skottowe Wannamaker to Frank P. Graham, August 3, 1938, Graham Papers, Series 1.1, 1938, folder 67; *New York Times*, September 6, 1938; Mark Ethridge to Howard W. Odum, October 24, 1938, Odum Papers, 1938, folder 446; Mertz, *New Deal Policy and Southern Rural Poverty*, 241 – 42.

tar the enterprise as "subversive." Its resolutions were literally all over the map, touching on topics as varied as federal aid to education, child labor, birth spacing, the Scottsboro case (a racial cause célèbre of the 1930s), and the U.S. House of Representatives' red-baiting Committee on Un-American Activities; by trying to cover everything at once, the Conference failed to do anything coherent. Its membership was inevitably "do-gooder" in character, with many academics and social workers and few businesspeople or farmers.

Most seriously, the Birmingham Conference ran aground on the rock that the authors of the *Report* had sought to avoid: the race question. Its membership included such notable southern blacks as college presidents Charles S. Johnson, Benjamin E. Mays, and Mary McLeod Bethune; such interracial meetings were not unknown even in the Jim Crow era, but the high profile of the Birmingham assembly attracted the attention of the city's notorious Commissioner of Public Safety, Eugene ("Bull") Connor, who demanded that it conform to the city's segregation ordinance. After some turmoil, the meeting complied, but not without vigorous protest; The delegates pointedly resolved to hold no future meetings in any city requiring segregation. The conference subsequently passed a resolution condemning city officials and instructing the officers of the contemplated permanent body to keep future meetings both unsegregated and unmolested by segregationists. The controversy and resolution that was passed quickly became the defining qualities of the conference in the eyes of the public, providing reactionaries the ammunition they needed to discredit both the movement and the concerns that gave rise to it. The hopes of the NEC *Report* writers that southerners would place common regional loyalties over racial divisions collapsed in the face of the segregationist assault.[46]

The SCHW was not the only effort to propose systematic solutions to the ills described in the *Report.* Soon after the Birmingham meeting Barry Bingham and Mark Ethridge, in consultation with Francis Miller of the Southern Policy Committee, organized a meeting in Atlanta in January 1939. The thirty-two attendees included many who had also been in Birmingham, but the Atlanta group was deliberately less inclusive and

---

[46] Leading general accounts of the Birmingham Conference include those in Thomas A. Krueger, *And Promises to Keep: The Southern Conference for Human Welfare, 1938–1948* (Nashville, Tenn.: Vanderbilt University Press, 1967), 20–39, and Linda Reed, *Simple Decency and Common Sense: The Southern Conference Movement, 1938–1963* (Bloomington: Indiana University Press, 1991), 2–19. See also *Report of Proceedings of the Southern Conference for Human Welfare, Birmingham, Alabama, November 20–23, 1938,* esp. 13–22. On the Conference's effectiveness as a response to the *Report*, see Mertz, *New Deal Policy and Southern Rural Poverty,* 242–45.

more restrained. Its chief product, *A Working Economic Plan for the South*, concentrated on economic questions and on the development of five recommendations for federal action:

1. an expanded program of rural rehabilitation and resettlement;
2. expansion of federal public health programs, especially in the rural South;
3. federal aid to education, with provision for "equitable distribution between the races";
4. continued support for the rights of labor; and
5. an end to regional railroad freight differentials.

The group also endorsed a series of proposals for state action, most strikingly the abolition of the poll tax, a fixed levy on adults whose payment was a precondition for voting. Finally, in view of the long-run character of southern problems, the group endorsed a longstanding proposal of Howard Odum for a Council of Southern Regional Development, which in 1944 saw birth as the Southern Regional Council.[47] While the Atlanta group devised a reasonable, well focused, and coherent program, it lacked any formal standing to pursue it; its members were self-selected representatives of a southern liberalism that, with the waning of the New Deal and the waxing of southern white fears for the future of Jim Crow, was losing influence. Federal aid to education, a proposal with which Graham was closely identified, was repeatedly locked up in committees dominated by southern congressmen fearful of its impact on school segregation.[48] For the most part, their other proposals fared even worse.

The one major exception was the freight rate issue. As we have seen, the *Report* was most explicitly political when it decried "economic colonialism," and its assaults on alleged discriminatory treatment of the South were its most broadly popular features, even among many conservatives. But the moderate form of the argument was somewhat different from that which Foreman and his group had in mind. The writers of the *Report* somewhat naively believed all economic activity in the region to be in outside hands. Southern politicians, in particular, knew otherwise: While absentee owners held a number of chokepoints in the southern economy, a large group of indigenous entrepreneurs had developed by the 1930s, a

[47] Mertz, *New Deal Policy and Southern Rural Poverty*, 245 – 47; Mark Ethridge to Frank P. Graham, November 30, 1938, Graham Papers, Series 1.1, 1938, folder 78; Howard W. Odum to Graham, December 9, 1938, Graham Papers, Series 1.1, 1938, folder 80; "A Working Economic Plan for the South: Recommendations adopted at Atlanta, Ga., January 13, 1939" (Washington, D.C.: National Policy Committee, 1939), copy in SCHW Papers.
[48] Tindall, *Emergence of the New South*, 496 – 97.

class that was eager to break the remaining grip of outsiders and free up the flow of commerce. While otherwise having little in common with the New Dealers and their allies among organized labor and blacks, these businessmen were perfectly happy to see a sustained regional assault on structural disabilities. Of these impediments the one most amenable to alteration was the chronically discriminatory structure of regional railroad freight rates. Railroads were heavily regulated, and thus vulnerable to political attack; moreover, a regional political organization, the Southern Governors' Conference, formed in 1934 in order to make the fight for rate equalization.[49]

The governors were eager to take up the *Report* as grist for their mill, even to the point of broadening their interests to include a comprehensive ten-year program of economic development. The proposal, drafted in December 1939 by a committee headed by Clarence Poe of the *Progressive Farmer*, laid out ten points, which collectively amounted to yet another call for a better balance between agriculture and industry. The program was effectively stillborn, however; the governors lacked sustained interest, obsessed as they were with freight rate equalization and, soon, with securing war industry for their states. Their apathy was unfortunate, for they could have provided what the SCHW's activists and Odum's reformers could not: a true regional political vehicle through which the concerns of the *Report* could be addressed. Instead, they pursued what subsequent analysts agree was a minor issue, one whose overtones of sectional conflict made it symbolically attractive but whose actual contribution to regional welfare was slight.[50]

Thus the major southern responses to the *Report* dissolved in controversy, foundered on the race issue, or led to dead ends. Moreover, the *Report* itself was overtaken by events that quickly rendered it outdated. First, of course, came the Second World War. As we have already seen, its mere prospect cast a shadow over any domestic policy initiatives in the late 1930s. The military buildup after 1939 and America's entry into the war in December 1941 flooded the region, like the nation, with change, rendering obsolete the concerns that had dominated just several years before. Unemployment and underemployment vanished; displaced rural peoples flocked to work at war plants in mushrooming cities; the massive federal aid that reformers had hoped for in the late 1930s flowed in under entirely different auspices now, as military payrolls, as investment in war plants, and as payment for supplies.

---

[49] On freight rates, see Tindall, *Emergence of the New South*, 599 – 604; Joubert, *Southern Freight Rates in Transition*.

[50] Mertz, *New Deal Policy and Southern Rural Poverty*, 247 – 51.

The postwar years continued what one historian has termed "the improbable era." In contrast to earlier demobilizations, no depression ensued; rather, the longest, strongest economic upsurge in world history gathered steam, not to run its course until the early 1970s. National prosperity underwrote major transitions in the southern economy that had seemed impossible but a few years earlier; rural migration to the North and West burgeoned, as the pressure of farm mechanization was compensated for by the expansion of industrial jobs in Detroit, Chicago, and Los Angeles. Those jobs were supplemented by southern industrial jobs; "footloose" industries quickened their pace to southward, while fuller utilization of plant capacity unused in the 1930s ushered in a boom in construction of branch plants, of which the South received more than its share. Industrialization was aided by the elaboration of state development programs far beyond the scope of Mississippi's BAWI program, and by a permanently enlarged federal presence, notably in defense. Southeastern per capita income, stuck at half the U.S. average since 1880, began to converge upon national levels after 1940, reaching roughly 88 percent by 1990.[51]

Finally, and less happily, the old nemesis of regionalist reformers, the race issue, which had been relatively muted in the emergency times of the 1930s, became an all-devouring obsession of southern whites after the late 1940s. In the postwar climate of southern white "massive resistance" to racial reform, the southern liberal notion of a common interest uniting all southerners, or, in its more radical version, a class-based coalition of the white and black poor against the rich, fell victim of the older insistence that blacks and whites had separate destinies and that the merest suggestion to the contrary was tantamount to treason to the (white) "South." The race issue likewise became central to southern liberals, who increasingly found that only those willing to enter the lists against segregation and discrimination could continue to bear the name. Some old liberals, such as the Richmond journalist Virginius Dabney, whose desire for regional progress was wedded to continuing faith in the nostrums of "separate but equal," sadly found themselves forced to join the conservatives. Others, more willing to accept the need to end segregation, found they were losing old southern white allies even while forging stronger ties to blacks and northern white liberals. Emblematic of the shift was that of Odum's Southern Regional Council, which after

---

[51] On the wartime and postwar eras, see Schulman, *From Cotton Belt to Sunbelt;* Charles P. Roland, *The Improbable Era: The South since World War II* (Lexington: University Press of Kentucky, 1975); David R. Goldfield, *Promised Land: The South since 1945* (Arlington Heights, Ill.: Harlan Davidson, 1987).

several years of vain effort to maintain its focus on regional development transformed itself into the central clearinghouse for white liberal supporters of civil rights; as Foreman explained it later, it "just [didn't] seem to be possible to do anything in the South until you face[d] the race question."[52]

In retrospect, of course, the racial obsessions of what we now call the Civil Rights Era were unavoidable, and the new willingness of southern liberals to advocate a complete end to segregation and disfranchisement was important to the final overthrow of Jim Crow in the 1960s. Nonetheless, it came at a price: The regionalist vision, which was at least implicitly interracial, was supplanted by a racially bifurcated construction of the South, one in which whites implicitly limited "southern identity" to themselves and blacks were at best ambivalent about considering themselves "southern" at all. The resulting divisions, with the obstacles they have posed to coordinated assault on the continuing problems of the South, haunt the region to this day.

THE REPORT IN MODERN PERSPECTIVE

Over half a century has now passed since the *Report,* an epoch of sometimes breathtaking change in the South. Younger southerners living in the modern suburbs of Atlanta, or North Carolina's Research Triangle, or Orlando, or the Dallas – Fort Worth "Metroplex," can be forgiven for wondering how the South in which they live could ever have been described in such grim terms, or how its problems could have seemed so intractable. In part this reflects our inevitable difficulty in seeing through the eyes of others, especially those living in the past. But it also reflects some important problems with the *Report* itself, problems clarified not only by historical experience but by subsequent thinking about the problems of economic underdevelopment.

While the *Report* presented itself as a simple description of the realities of southern poverty, underlying it was an argument about the causes of that poverty. The argument was organized around two key ideas: "low purchasing power" and "economic colonialism." In various forms these concepts offered much insight into the southern malady, and continue to be used in sundry ways by historians and social scientists even today. But

[52]The postwar political shift is covered in Numan V. Bartley and Hugh Davis Graham, *Southern Politics and the Second Reconstruction* (Baltimore: Johns Hopkins University Press, 1975); the story of southern liberalism during and after World War II is discussed in Sosna, *In Search of the Silent South,* 105 – 71.

their use by the authors of the *Report* was unsophisticated. Non-economists for the most part, eager to reach a mass audience, the authors offered simple diagnoses of the South's problems, diagnoses that understated the difficulties that would be faced in solving them.

First, let us consider their stress on "purchasing power." At times they suggested an explanation that later theorists of economic development would dub "circular and cumulative causation," the notion that the great weight of southern poverty was self-generating and self-perpetuating.[53] Thus low wages for workers in southern manufacturing were enforced by job competition from masses of desperately poor rural southerners, who in turn faced a bleak choice between employment in a backward agriculture sector or no employment at all. Poor education and health — inadequate development of human capabilities, or what economists call "human capital" investment — were both cause and product of poverty. Such stubborn, interlocking problems required a radical external shock to break up the vicious cycles.

Ironically, at the time the *Report* was being written, such shocks were already hammering at the system. The Depression and New Deal farm programs had led to the collapse of the old agricultural regime, pushing sharecroppers off the land and even out of the region, while pressing their landlords to mechanize. The shocks of the Second World War and the postwar era completed what was begun in the 1930s.[54] To observers at the time, however, the changes of the 1930s were only deepening the immiseration of a southern peasantry; concerned with the despair before them, they sought both shock and amelioration from the same source: the federal government. Implicitly (and, in the preliminary draft, explicitly) the authors of the *Report* hoped for a massive infusion of aid for the poorest southerners, at once remedying the poverty of the masses and "priming the pump" of southern economic growth.

As outlined above, the *Report*'s "low purchasing power" diagnosis captured well the dilemmas of persistent southern poverty; indeed, it anticipates some of the more sophisticated modern interpretations of the pre – World War II southern economy.[55] However, at times the *Report* framed its analysis in a form at once less dire and less sophisticated. This was the case in the *Report*'s discussion of regional wage differentials. In

---

[53] See for instance, Gunnar Myrdal, *Rich Lands and Poor: The Road to World Prosperity* (New York: Harper & Row, 1957); Albert O. Hirschman, *The Strategy of Economic Development* (New Haven, Conn.: Yale University Press, 1958).

[54] For a discussion of these shocks, see Gavin Wright, *Old South, New South: Revolutions in the Southern Economy since the Civil War* (New York: Basic Books, 1986), 198 – 274.

[55] Wright, *Old South, New South.*

part because the *Report* was composed against the background of debate over the Fair Labor Standards Act, it tended to see low manufacturing wages, not as part of an interlocking economic pathology, but as an independent cause, one readily remedied by simple political means — minimum wages, encouragement of unionization, the election of more liberal officials by an enfranchised electorate. Advocates of this position argued that eliminating low-wage labor would force southern businesses to upgrade their investments in plant, equipment, and "human capital," thus in the longer term replacing low-wage jobs with high-wage ones. However, raising industrial wages by law as a means of attacking southern poverty might well have had a less happy effect, setting in motion a train of consequences — failed businesses, workers let go, opportunities for new enterprises closed off — that might have exacerbated the problem the law was intended to solve. Of course, with the passage of the FLSA the experiment was launched; but the legislation failed to reach most southern workers, its enforcers were slow in developing standards for those industries that were covered, and wartime labor shortages soon sent wage rates well above the mandated floors. The postwar boom further obscured the picture: Did the minimum wage improve the positions of southern workers, or would prosperity have lifted them in any case? Did increases in employment show that the minimum wage would not have hurt southern employment, or simply that postwar expansion more than compensated for the damage the minimums caused?[56] The developmental impact of the minimum wage remains unclear; but most economists today are skeptical of the ability of minimum wages, or any other such direct government interferences with market mechanisms, to raise workers' incomes without having adverse effects on employment.

As with "low purchasing power," the attribution of southern economic ills to "colonialism" contains much insight; indeed, it has subsequently formed the basis for a broad range of economic development theories concerned with the role of "dependency" in producing or perpetuating underdevelopment. But, especially in light of subsequent history, the hostility of the *Report* to absentee control of the South's industry, re-

<hr>

[56] On the inadequate coverage of the FLSA, see Fraser, *Labor Will Rule*, 411 – 12. An extended discussion of regional wage differentials, federal labor policy, and related matters appears in Calvin B. Hoover and B. U. Ratchford, *Economic Resources and Policies of the South* (New York: Macmillan, 1951), 393 – 421. A review of the literature on the impact of the FLSA on southern industry appears in Clarence H. Danhof, "Four Decades of Thought on the South's Economic Problems," in *Essays in Southern Economic Development,* ed. Melvin L. Greenhut and W. Tate Whitman (Chapel Hill: University of North Carolina Press, 1964), 7 – 68, esp. 58 – 60. For the impact of the FLSA on a major southern industry, see James A. Hodges, *New Deal Labor Policy and the Southern Cotton Textile Industry* (Knoxville: University of Tennessee Press, 1986), 180 – 90.

sources, and credit, and the alarms it raised over discriminatory treatment of the region, are the least enduring features of its analysis. Few analysts now believe, as many did in the 1930s, that Birmingham, Alabama, could have competed with Pittsburgh as a steelmaking center had it not been stifled by the United States Steel Corporation; fewer still would contend that in the absence of outside infusions of capital and entrepreneurship the region would have developed as well as it has since World War II. Protective tariffs, to be sure, did have sectionally discriminatory effects, although these were already fading as the southern economy was losing its traditional export orientation. Regional freight rate differentials were of some consequence, chiefly because they tended to lock into place existing geographic patterns of economic activity and thus posed obstacles to the development of new southern industries. However, they were no problem to existing producers, who negotiated favorable rates with the carriers; and the changing structure of the nation's transportation system (notably the construction of highways and the rise of trucking) was rapidly nullifying the effect of the old rate system. In sum, "colonialism" was useful more as a political rallying cry than as an analysis.[57]

If the *Report* can be faulted for the flaws in its central theses, it can likewise be criticized for the factors it glossed over or ignored. Foremost among these surely was its failure to confront the impact of racial oppression on southern poverty. One black writer, commenting on the *Report,* contended that the root of southern poverty lay in "the obsession that the labor of the Negro should be compensated only to the point of bare subsistence." This practice not only deprived a large proportion of the southern population of needed purchasing power, but, in accordance with the "iron law of wages," tended to depress white incomes as well. Racism arguably had more profound effects as well: By arbitrarily denying access to human capital development and entrepreneurial opportunity for a large segment of the southern population, it also deprived the South of resources valuable to the growth of the economy as a whole, while deepening long-term problems still all too visible in pockets such as the Mississippi Delta and the Alabama Black Belt. If "low purchasing power" was one of the central southern ills, the artificial restriction of that purchasing power on the basis of skin color exacerbated the problem.[58] Yet none of

---

[57] A devastating critique of the "colonial economy" argument is Clarence H. Danhof, "Four Decades of Thought," 30 – 51.

[58] "America's Number 1 Problem," *Opportunity: Journal of Negro Life* 16 (August 1938): 228 – 29. A comprehensive discussion of the effect of racism on the southern economy appears in Roger L. Ransom and Richard Sutch, *One Kind of Freedom: The Economic Consequences of Emancipation* (New York: Cambridge University Press, 1977), 176 – 86.

these issues received serious attention in the *Report*. As we have seen, there were good political and intellectual reasons for its neglect of the peculiar burdens of race; nonetheless, an observer in the 1990s can only count it a grievous omission.

Another serious deficiency of the *Report*, related to its embrace of the "colonial" thesis, is its neglect of the role of southern entrepreneurship. All too often in its pages, the South appears as a passive victim of malevolent forces, or persons, beyond its control. While the published *Report* did concede the existence of a native class of textile industrialists, even that acknowledgment was a late, grudging addition to a draft that implicitly depicted entrepreneurship as a Yankee monopoly. Here the drafters of the *Report* displayed some social myopia. Disproportionately drawn from academe, the federal bureaucracy, and the philanthropic establishment, they were relatively unacquainted with the business resources of the South; Foreman, in particular, was convinced, falsely, that all business criticism of the *Report* had "almost uniformly come from agents of northern-controlled corporations."[59] This naiveté had two serious consequences: It tended to overestimate the need for federal intervention to supply growth that southerners could not supply themselves, and it cut off the *Report*'s drafters from potential allies in the southern business community. In the longer term, it contributed to the most important limitation of the *Report* for our time: its failure to foresee the path the South would ultimately take out of the impasse of the 1930s. For, while injections of federal spending materially aided the South in its post-1945 economic resurgence, the central role was nonetheless played by the region's own supply of entrepreneurial talent, building on older achievements and exploiting the opportunities presented by the postwar boom. The *Report*'s neglect of the potential of southerners to be agents of their own redemption represents perhaps its most egregious failure.

From fifty years' vantage, the *Report on Economic Conditions of the South* shows defects of commission and omission, of conceptual and empirical understanding, about the situation it sought to illuminate. Despite all these problems, however, after half a century the *Report* holds up remarkably well. At its best, it offers a discussion of the economic dilemmas facing the South of the 1930s unparalleled in its clarity and comprehensiveness. Nowhere else can one find so concise an overview of southern poverty, or one so appreciative of the depth of the problem. Moreover, while fifty years of progress have obscured the South of the *Report* with an overlay of asphalt, glossy downtowns, and comfortable

[59] Clark Foreman to George Biggers, January 6, 1939, SCHW Papers.

suburbs, much of that old, ramshackle world remains to be seen by those who leave the interstate highways at the appropriate exits, and large numbers of southerners still display in their lives the scarred legacy of that age. Finally, the writers of the *Report* did their literary job awfully well. When Lowell Mellett submitted it to Franklin Roosevelt, he warned him, "Do not read it for literature, for it is not that."[60] Precious in style it certainly is not; but as honest description, it reveals its subject matter with simplicity and transparency. In the *Report* we see the South of the late 1930s in the depth of its plight: not through a glass darkly, but face to face.

---

[60] Lowell Mellett to Franklin D. Roosevelt, August 6, 1938, Franklin Delano Roosevelt Papers, Official File 788, Franklin D. Roosevelt Library, Hyde Park, N.Y.

PART TWO

The Document

Report on Economic Conditions of the South

REQUEST FOR REPORT

The White House
Washington, June 22, 1938

My Dear Mr. Mellett:

Discussions in Congress and elsewhere in connection with legislation affecting the economic welfare of the Nation have served to point out the differences in the problems and needs of the different sections of the country and have indicated the advisability of a clear and concise statement of these needs and problems in a form readily available, not only to the Members of Congress, but to the public generally.

Attention has recently been focused particularly upon the South in connection with the wages and hours bill, and I should like the National Emergency Council to undertake the preparation of such a statement of the problems and needs of the South. In preparing this statement I suggest that you call freely upon the various governmental departments and administrative agencies for information as to matters with which they are especially acquainted, and also that you request the assistance of southerners well known for their interest in the South and familiarity with its problems.

The outcome of this undertaking may indicate the advisability of similar studies with reference to other sections of the country.

Very sincerely,

(Signed) Franklin D. Roosevelt

Hon. Lowell Mellett
Executive Director
National Emergency Council

The National Emergency Council, *Report on Economic Conditions of the South* (Washington, D.C.: Government Printing Office, 1938).

THE PRESIDENT'S LETTER

To the Members of the Conference on Economic Conditions in the South:

No purpose is closer to my heart at this moment than that which caused me to call you to Washington. That purpose is to obtain a statement — or perhaps, I should say a restatement as of today — of the economic conditions of the South, a picture of the South in relation to the rest of the country, in order that we may do something about it; in order that we may not only carry forward the work that has been begun toward the rehabilitation of the South, but that the program of such work may be expanded in the directions that this new presentation shall indicate.

My intimate interest in all that concerns the South is, I believe, known to all of you; but this interest is far more than a sentimental attachment born of a considerable residence in your section and of close personal friendship for so many of your people. It proceeds even more from my feeling of responsibility toward the whole Nation. It is my conviction that the South presents right now the Nation's No. 1 economic problem — the Nation's problem, not merely the South's. For we have an economic unbalance in the Nation as a whole, due to this very condition of the South.

It is an unbalance that can and must be righted, for the sake of the South and of the Nation.

Without going into the long history of how this situation came to be — the long and ironic history of the despoiling of this truly American section of the country's population — suffice it for the immediate purpose to get a clear perspective of the task that is presented to us. That task embraces the wasted or neglected resources of land and water, the abuses suffered by the soil, the need for cheap fertilizer and cheap power; the problems presented by the population itself — a population still holding the great heritages of King's Mountain and Shiloh[1] — the problems presented by the South's capital resources and the absentee ownership of those resources, and problems growing out of the new industrial era and, again, of absentee ownership of the new industries. There is the

---

[1] The Revolutionary Battle of King's Mountain, fought October 7, 1780, on the North Carolina-South Carolina line, saw the defeat of a force of British regulars by patriot militia composed of "over-mountain men" from present-day East Tennessee. On April 6 – 7, 1862, at the battle of Shiloh, in West Tennessee, one of the hardest-fought battles of the American Civil War, the Confederate army of Tennessee nearly threw back an invading Union Army that had hitherto met with little opposition. Roosevelt invoked these "great heritages" to establish the old-stock American credentials of poor (implicitly white) southerners. To a society that still regarded whites as superior to nonwhites and harbored lingering suspicions of late-arriving immigrants as somehow deficient in intelligence, morals, and American patriotism, Roosevelt implied that the problems of southern poverty, disease, and illiteracy were the products of environment, not personal or racial failure, and thus deserved sympathy, not ridicule.

problem of labor and employment in the South and the related problem of protecting women and children in this field. There is the problem of farm ownership, of which farm tenantry is a part, and of farm income. There are questions of taxation, of education, of housing, and of health.

More and more definitely in recent years those in the South who have sought selflessly to evaluate the elements constituting the general problem, have come to agree on certain basic factors. I have asked Mr. Mellett to present for your consideration a statement of these factors as prepared by various departments of the Government. I ask you to consider this statement critically, in the light of your own general or specific knowledge, in order that it may be made representative of the South's own best thought and that it may be presented to Congress and the public as such.

I had hoped to attend your meeting and listen to your discussions. Unhappily, other pressing work makes this impossible. Please accept my sincere regret that I cannot be with you, and be assured that I anticipate with deep interest the result of your labors.

Franklin D. Roosevelt

The White House
Washington, D.C., July 5, 1938

LETTER OF TRANSMITTAL

July 25, 1938

To the President:

In response to your request of June 22, 1938, there is transmitted herewith a report on the economic problems of the South.

The report presents in only a small degree the manifold assets and advantages possessed by the South, being concerned primarily not with what the South has, but with what the South needs.

Preparation of the report was aided by the counsel of an advisory committee of southern citizens known for their interest in the region and their familiarity with its problems. It is their expressed hope and belief that the South will benefit from a thorough examination of the factors that have produced the present economic unbalance, hurtful not only to their section but to the country as a whole. This committee included:

Dr. B. F. Ashe, president, University of Miami, Miami, Fla.; Governor Carl Bailey, Little Rock, Ark.; Barry Bingham, publisher, Louisville Courier Journal, Louisville, Ky.; W. B. Bizzell, president, State University, Norman, Okla.; Col. P. H. Callahan, president, Louisville Varnish Co., Louisville, Ky.; L. O. Crosby, lumberman, Picayune,

Miss.; Judge Blanton Fortson, judge, superior court, Athens, Ga.; Frank Graham, president, University of North Carolina, Chapel Hill, N. C.; Attorney James Hammond, past president, Chamber of Commerce, Columbia, S. C.; Col. Leroy Hodges, State comptroller, Richmond, Va.; Miss Lucy Randolph Mason, C. I. O. representative, Atlanta, Ga.; H. L. Mitchell, secretary-treasurer, Southern Tenant Farmers Union, Memphis, Tenn.; Gen. John C. Persons, president, First National Bank, Birmingham, Ala.; Prof. Chas. W. Pipkin, Louisiana State University, Baton Rouge, La.; Paul Poynter, publisher, St. Petersburg Times, St. Petersburg, Fla.; J. H. Reynolds, president, Hendricks College, Conway, Ark.; Robert J. Smith, vice president, Braniff Airways, Dallas, Tex.; S. L. Smith, Peabody College, Nashville, Tenn.; Alexander Speer, former president, Virginia Public Service Co., Alexandria, Va.; Joseph G. Tillman, planter, Statesboro, Ga.; J. Skottowe Wannamaker, president, American Cotton Association, St. Matthews, S. C.; Carl White, A. F. of L., Port Arthur, Tex.

The various departments and administrative agencies were called on for information. Factual statements were checked by the Central Statistical Board, and many men and women in the Government contributed their knowledge and efforts. The actual drafting of the 15 sections of the report was the work of southerners, intimately acquainted with their own region and vitally concerned in its welfare.

As used in this report, the term "the Southeast" includes the States of Virginia, Kentucky, Tennessee, North Carolina, South Carolina, Georgia, Florida, Alabama, Mississippi, Louisiana and Arkansas; the "Southwest" means Oklahoma and Texas, and "The South" covers all the 13 States.

Effort has been made to meet your desire for a concise statement. The report therefore does not attempt to be exhaustive. On any one of the 15 topics discussed much more extensive treatment can be found in official Government reports or in studies that have been made by educational institutions and individuals.

One thing appears to be made clear when the principal difficulties faced by the South are brought into perspective and when what the South has to offer the Nation is laid alongside what the South needs for its own people; that is that the economic problems of the South are not beyond the power of men to solve. Another thing made clear, however, is that there is no simple solution. The solution must be part political, with the Federal Government participating along with state, county, city, town, and township government. But there must be participation also by industry, business and schools — and by citizens, South and North.

The example given by the men named above in lending their time and their patient consideration to the material condensed into this brief report seems to assure that the citizens of the South do not hesitate to face the facts of the present situation. This, in turn, would seem to assure — to use your own language — that something will be done about it.

Lowell Mellett
The Executive Director
National Emergency Council

SECTIONS OF REPORT

1. Economic resources.
2. Soil.
3. Water.
4. Population.
5. Private and public income.
6. Education.
7. Health.
8. Housing.
9. Labor.
10. Women and children.
11. Ownership and use of land.
12. Credit.
13. Use of natural resources.
14. Industry.
15. Purchasing power.

SECTION 1. ECONOMIC RESOURCES

In the South, as elsewhere, the two most important economic endowments are its people and its physical resources. The 1937 census estimates showed that the 13 Southern States had more than 36 million persons. While this population is descended from the peoples of virtually every country of the world, a larger percentage derives from early American stock than that of any other region in the United States; 97.8 percent, according to the last census, was native born; 71 percent white, and 29 percent colored.

The birthrate in the South exceeds that of any other region, and the excess of births over deaths makes the South the most fertile source for replenishing the population of the United States. At a time when the population of the country as a whole is becoming stationary, there is a continuous stream of people leaving the South to work in other parts of the Nation — greatly in excess of the corresponding migration to the South.

The South is a huge crescent embracing 552 million acres in 13 States from Virginia on the east to Texas on the west. It has widely varying topographic conditions — vast prairies, wooded plains, fertile valleys, and the highest mountains in the eastern United States.

The transportation facilities of the South are, for the most part, excellent. It is covered by rail lines which connect the interior with ports and give easy access to other regions. Both the Mississippi and the Ohio rivers' navigation facilities serve the South. The Warrior-Tombigbee system taps the important industrial region around Birmingham, while the Tennessee River system, now being developed by the Tennessee Valley Authority, will bring water transportation to the very heart of the Southeast. The highways of the South are well advanced. Roads are built cheaply and are usable in all seasons. The region is well served by airlines. Bordered by both the Atlantic and the Gulf, the South has ideal harbors and many fine ports. Trade with Europe has been important for three centuries. Across the Gulf and Caribbean the South can expect further trade development.

The South has been richly endowed with physical resources. No other region offers such diversity of climate and soil. With a climate ranging from temperate to subtropical, nearly half of that part of the country where there is a frostless growing season for more than 6 months of the year is in the South. Throughout almost the entire South there is ample annual rainfall and little artificial irrigation is required.

The soils of the South are the most widely varied of the Nation. Alabama, a typical southern State, has 7 major types and almost 300 soil subtypes. These soils permit the growing of a wide variety of products: cotton, tobacco, grains, fruits, melons, vegetables, potatoes, hay, nuts, sugar cane, and hemp. The South leads the world in production of cotton and tobacco.

Soil and climate combine to give it forests of many kinds. With 40 percent of the Nation's forests, the South has found its woodlands second only to cotton as a source of wealth. Approximately 30 percent of the land is still in forests. Despite exploitation and abuse, forests still cover almost 200,000,000 acres, and more than half of the country's second-growth saw timber is in the South.

The region leads the world in naval stores production. Because southern pine reseeds itself and grows rapidly, the South has great potentialities for the production of paper.

The South lags, however, in the production of livestock, despite its wealth of grasslands. Its 20,000,000 cattle amount to less than a third of the total found on American farms; and because of the poor quality of many of them, the value of the annual production of cattle is only one-sixth of the nation's total.

Fish and game are as plentiful as in any part of the country. Louisiana is our largest raw fur producer.

The South has more than 300 different minerals: asbestos, asphalt, barite, bauxite, clays, coal, diamonds, feldspar, fluorspar, gypsum, lead, limestone, marble, mercury, phosphate rock, pyrites, salt, sand and gravel, silica, sulfur, zinc, and so on by the scores.

With less than 2 percent of its seams so far tapped, the Southeast contains a fifth of the Nation's soft coal. It mines a full tenth of our iron ore annually, but it produces only slightly more than 7 percent of our pig iron.

The South possesses approximately 27 percent of the Nation's installed hydroelectric generating capacity, although it produces only 21 percent of the electric power annually generated. The region contains 13 percent of the country's undeveloped hydroelectric power.

Nearly two-thirds of the Nation's crude oil is produced in the South, and over two-thirds of our supply of natural gas comes from southern fields. In 1935 the South furnished about half of the country's marble output. Florida and Tennessee produce 97 percent of all our phosphates, and Texas and Louisiana supply over 99 percent of our sulfur.

Commercial fisheries flourish on both the Atlantic and Gulf coasts. Shore fisheries engaged in taking oysters, clams, menhaden, mackerel, sponges, and shrimp are especially important.

In spite of this wealth of population and natural resource, the South is poor in the machinery for converting this wealth to the uses of its people. With 28 percent of the Nation's population, it has only 16 percent of the tangible assets, including factories, machines, and the tools with which people make their living. With more than half the country's farmers, the South has less than a fifth of the farm implements. Despite its coal, oil, gas, and water power, the region uses only 15 percent of the Nation's factory horsepower. Its potentialities have been neglected and its opportunities unrealized.

The paradox of the South is that while it is blessed by Nature with immense wealth, its people as a whole are the poorest in the country. Lacking industries of its own, the South has been forced to trade the richness of its soil, its minerals and forests, and the labor of its people for goods manufactured elsewhere. If the South received such goods in sufficient quantity to meet its needs, it might consider itself adequately paid.

SECTION 2. SOIL

Nature gave the South good soil. With less than a third of the Nation's area, the South contains more than a third of the Nation's good farming acreage. It has two-thirds of all the land in America receiving a 40-inch annual rainfall or better. It has nearly half of the land on which crops can grow for 6 months without danger of frost.

This heritage has been sadly exploited. Sixty-one percent of all the Nation's land badly damaged by erosion is in the Southern States. An expanse of southern farm land as large as South Carolina has been gullied and washed away; at least 22 million acres of once fertile soil has been ruined beyond repair. Another area the size of Oklahoma and Alabama combined has been seriously damaged by erosion. In addition, the sterile sand and gravel washed off this land has covered over a fertile valley acreage equal in size to Maryland.

There are a number of reasons for this wastage:

Much of the South's land originally was so fertile that it produced crops for many years no matter how carelessly it was farmed. For generations thousands of southern farmers plowed their furrows up and down the slopes, so that each furrow served as a ditch to hasten the runoff of silt-laden water after every rain. While many farmers have now learned the importance of terracing their land or plowing it on the contours, thousands still follow the destructive practices of the past.

Half of the South's farmers are tenants, many of whom have little interest in preserving soil they do not own.

The South's chief crops are cotton, tobacco, and corn; all of these are intertilled crops — the soil is plowed between the rows, so that it is left loose and bare of vegetation.

The topsoil washes away much more swiftly than from land planted to cover crops, such as clover, soybeans, and small grains. Moreover, cotton, tobacco, and corn leave few stalks and leaves to be plowed under in the fall; and as a result the soil constantly loses its humus and its capacity to absorb rainfall.

Even after harvest, southern land is seldom planted to cover crops which would protect it from the winter rains. This increases erosion tenfold.

Southeastern farms are the smallest in the Nation. The operating units average only 71 acres, and nearly one-fourth of them are smaller than 20 acres. A farmer with so little land is forced to plant every foot of it in cash crops; he cannot spare an acre for soil restoring crops or pasture. Under the customary tenancy system, moreover, he has every incentive to plant all his land to crops which will bring in the largest possible immediate cash return. The landlord often encourages him in this destructive practice of cash-cropping.

Training in better agricultural methods, such as planting soil-restoring crops, terracing, contour-plowing, and rotation, has been spreading, but such training is still unavailable to most southern farmers. Annually the South spends considerably more money for fertilizer than for agricultural training through its land-grant colleges,[2] experiment stations, and extension workers.

Forests are one of the best protections against erosion. Their foliage breaks the force of the rain; their roots bind the soil so that it cannot wash away; their fallen leaves form a blanket of vegetable cover which soaks up the water and checks runoff. Yet the South has cut away a large part of its forest, leaving acres of gullied, useless soil. There has been comparatively little effort at systematic reforestation. Overgrazing, too, has resulted in serious erosion throughout the Southwest.

There is a close relationship between this erosion and floods, which recently have been causing a loss to the Nation estimated at about $35,000,000 annually. Rainfall runs off uncovered land much more rapidly than it does from land planted to cover crops or forest. Recent studies indicate that a single acre of typical corn land lost approximately 127,000 more gallons of rainfall in a single year than a similar field planted to grass. Another experiment showed that land sodded in grass lost less than 1 percent of a heavy rain through immediate runoff, while nearby land planted to cotton lost 31 percent. In short, unprotected land not only is in danger of destruction; it also adds materially to the destructive power of the swollen streams into which it drains.

These factors — each one reenforcing all the others — are causing an unparalleled wastage of the South's most valuable asset, its soil. They are steadily cutting down its agricultural income, and steadily adding to its cost of production as compared with other areas of the world which raise the same crops.

For example, it takes quantities of fertilizer to make worn-out, eroded land produce. The South, with only one-fifth of the Nation's income, pays three-fifths of the Nation's fertilizer bill. In 1929 it bought 5½ million tons of commercial fertilizer at a cost of $161,000,000. And although fertilizer performs a valuable and necessary service, it does not restore the soil. For a year or two it may nourish a crop, but the land still produces meagerly and at high cost.

Moreover, southern farmers cannot pile on fertilizer fast enough to put back the essential minerals which are washing out of their land. Each year, about 27,500,000 tons of nitrogen and phosphorus compounds are leached out of southern soil and sent down the rivers to the sea.

---

[2] The Morrill Act of 1862 granted each state 30,000 acres of federal land to serve as an endowment for at least one agricultural college. The resulting "land-grant colleges" have since played enormous roles in developing and disseminating new plant and animal varieties and modern agricultural technology and practices. Sometimes ridiculed as "cow colleges," many now rank among the leading American state universities.

The South is losing more than $300,000,000 worth of fertile topsoil through erosion every year. This is not merely a loss of income — it is a loss of irreplaceable capital.

SECTION 3. WATER

The water resources of the South are abundant. Except on its western fringe, it is generously supplied with waters for municipal use, for electric power, for navigation, and for crop production. Inefficient control or use of these waters has impaired their value in some areas, while in other areas their very superabundance has retarded economic development.

Many communities need better systems of public water supply. In the coastal plain and in the States west of the Mississippi deep wells generally tap water of good quality. The quantity of such underground sources is ample for most communities, but in a number of instances they have been depleted by overdraft and by waste. With the exception of the seaports and older river ports, the larger southern cities and the industrial towns have grown up on the Piedmont and upland regions where groundwaters are more meager. Many are in headwater areas having only small stream-flow during the summer months. Pollution of such streams by cities and towns has impaired public health and has restricted their recreational and industrial use. In these and other areas insufficient provision has been made for waste disposal to keep the streams pure.

In much of the South the combination of heavy rainfall, relatively large stream flow, and favorable topography has made possible great developments of water power. Hydroelectric plants with an installed capacity of approximately 4 million horsepower have been constructed, and the resulting power is of vital importance to the southern economy. In 1937, hydroelectric developments in the Carolinas, Georgia, and Alabama supplied about 85 percent of all power produced for public utilities in that area; whereas hydroelectric power contributed only 37 percent of the total power produced for public utilities in the United States as a whole. Even greater resources lie undeveloped. It is estimated that the potential output of feasible undeveloped power sites in the South would be five times the hydroelectric power actually produced in 1937. These power reserves constitute a rich asset to be utilized as the markets of the South grow.

In the Mississippi Valley, along the Gulf coast and much of the South Atlantic coast, the settlement of the country followed the numerous waterways. Although the significance of river transportation is not generally recognized, it is of growing importance along the Mississippi River, on the Warrior-Tombigbee system, and in the extensive improvements in progress in the Tennessee Basin. An intracoastal waterway now provides a safe route for vessels of moderate draft along three-fourths of the southern coast. Channel deepening has provided free access for ocean shipping to such inland ports as Richmond, Jacksonville, Beaumont, and Houston.

Most sections receive adequate rainfall for crop production. Only 2,630,000 acres have been improved by irrigation. Of this acreage, some of the more prosperous part is used for vegetable, rice, and citrus-fruit production. In the semiarid western sections, except in the lower Rio Grande Valley, irrigation is in the developmental stage, and its economic possibilities have not been explored fully.

Throughout most of the South an overabundance, not scarcity, of water limits the agricultural use of fertile lands. By means of drainage more than 22,000,000 acres of wetland have been reclaimed. Some of these drained lands are the most fertile in the South, and they are capable of affording a refuge for farmers who have exhausted the eroding upland soils. Additional acreage can be brought to use as fast as the costs of drainage land-conditioning permit. However, a large part of the drained land now lies idle, and in some areas the drainage enterprises are poorly coordinated.

The settlement of wetlands has been retarded in part by malaria. The "fever" takes a heavy annual toll in human life and vitality. It is particularly widespread in those rural areas where drainage is inadequate.

Uncontrolled floodwaters likewise impose severe damages on the South. Much of its fertile farming land and many of its important cities lie within reach of floods. Vast sections of the alluvial valley of the Mississippi — 31,000 square miles of fertile land with a population of more than 2,000,000 — and numerous communities on other southern rivers, are within the danger zone. In the alluvial valley alone three-quarters of a million people were driven from their homes by the flood of 1927. Property damage from this flood was $220,000,000.

To consider another aspect of the South's water resources the once rich fisheries are being depleted, on the one hand, and the wildlife and recreational facilities developed only meagerly on the other. This is true notwithstanding that the shallow sounds along the coasts are important wintering grounds for game varieties of waterfowl and that the sport fishing along the coasts and in the inner sounds is truly notable.

In addition to their value as recreation grounds, these areas are also of tremendous importance as sources of seafood. But their value both as sources of food for the Nation and as a means of livelihood for those engaged in commercial fishing and shellfishing, is threatened by over-fishing and, in a few places, by water pollution.

The South is only now becoming aware of the fortune it has in its vast water resources — the value in transportation, power, fish, and game, and in health and recreation. It has just begun to consider the problems involved in conserving this many-sided resource, in curbing the destructive power of water and making it useful.

SECTION 4. POPULATION

The population of the South is growing more rapidly by natural increase than that of any other region. Its excess of births over deaths is 10 per thousand, as compared with the national average of 7 per thousand; and already it has the most thickly populated rural area in the United States. Of the 108,600,000 native-born persons in the country in 1930, 28,700,000 were born in the Southeast, all but 4,600,000 in rural districts.

These rural districts have exported one-fourth of their natural increase in sons and daughters. They have supplied their own growth, much of the growth of southern cities, and still have sent great numbers into other sections. Of these southerners born in rural areas, only 17,500,000 live in the locality where they were born, and 3,800,000 have left the South entirely.

This migration has taken from the South many of its ablest people. Nearly half of the eminent scientists born in the South are now living elsewhere. While some of these have been replaced by scientists from other sections of the country, the movement from the South has been much greater than this replacement. The search for wider opportunities than are available in the overcrowded, economically undeveloped southern communities drains away people from every walk of life. About one child of every eight born and educated in Alabama or Mississippi contributes his life's productivity to some other State.

The expanding southern population likewise has a marked effect on the South's economic standards. There are fewer productive adult workers and more dependents per capita than in other sections of the country. The export of population reflects the failure of the South to provide adequate opportunities for its people.

The largely rural States of the South must support nearly one-third of their population in school, while the industrial States support less than one-fourth. Moreover, in their search for jobs the productive middle-age groups leave the South in the greatest numbers, tending to make the South a land of the very old and the very young. A study of one southern community in 1928 showed that about 30 percent of the households were headed by women past middle age. Since 1930 most of these women, formerly able to live by odd jobs and gardening, have gone on relief. Relief studies in the eastern Cotton Belt have shown recently that 15 percent of the relief households were without a male over 16 years of age and 15 percent more, or 31 percent altogether, were without any employable male. Even if the southern workers were able, therefore, to secure wages equal to those of the North on a per capita basis dollar for dollar, a great gap would still remain between the living standards of southern families and those of other regions.

Recent figures indicate a slowing down of the migration to cities. In general, too, the rural population has increased most rapidly in those sections where the land is poorest. Thus the Appalachian and Ozark areas have shown a rapid increase, while the old black-belt cotton counties and Mississippi Delta counties have shown little or no gains. This has brought about an intensification of the problem of earning a living in the South.

Big families have been growing up on the average southern farm in recent generations. When the children reach maturity, either some of the older ones have to move away and find jobs in industry or trade, or the family farm — already too small — must be cut into smaller farms.

For many years after the War between the States, there was a general tendency to reduce the size of farms, but about 1910 a contrary movement began which partially offset this tendency. Nevertheless, because of the decrease in tillable land, in the older Southern States east of Texas, the farm acreage was actually less in 1930 than in 1860, though the rural population had nearly doubled. In 1930 there were nearly twice as many southern farms less than 20 acres in size as in 1880. These figures indicate serious maladjustment between the people and the land, and a consequent misuse of resources.

In certain sections there has been a tendency to revert to large plantations worked by machinery on an industrial basis. Tractors and gang plows are substituted for men and mules. This method of cutting operating costs also cuts the number of people needed for a given area of land or amount of crop. Farm unemployment constitutes a large proportion of the South's unemployment problem. This tendency is further disarranging the relationship between the people and the land. No longer owners, tenants, or croppers, the workers in these agricultural factories are more nearly day laborers — unskilled workers who can be hired one day and fired the next.

It has been estimated that nearly 3,000,000 young people matured into the 15 – 25 age group between 1930 and 1935 in the rural districts of 11 southeast States. Barely half a million took places left open by death; about the same number stayed in school; and the increase in number of farms, mostly subsistence farms, took care of about a quarter of a million. Remaining are some 1,750,000 who stay in the farm home as casual laborers or as unemployed.

Increasing competition for jobs has also upset the balance of employment between white and Negro. Unemployment among white people has caused them to seek jobs which were traditionally filled only by Negroes in the South. The field for the employment of Negroes has consequently been further constricted, causing greater migration. The lack of opportunity and the resulting job competition has lowered the living standards of both white and Negro workers in the South.

The population problems of the South — the disproportion of adult workers to dependents, the displacement of agricultural workers by machines, the substitution of white workers in traditionally Negro occupations, the emigration of skilled and educated productive workers — are the most pressing of any America must face. They are not local problems alone. With the South furnishing the basis for the population increase of the Nation, with southern workers coming into other sections of the country in quest of opportunity, with the South's large potential market for the Nation's goods, these problems are national.

SECTION 5. PRIVATE AND PUBLIC INCOME

The wealth of natural resources in the South — its forests, minerals, and fertile soil — benefit the South only when they can be turned into goods and services which its people need. So far the South has enjoyed relatively little of these benefits, simply because it has not had the money or credit to develop and purchase them.

Ever since the War between the States the South has been the poorest section of the Nation. The richest State in the South ranks lower in per capita income than the poorest State outside the region. In 1937 the average income in the South was $314; in the rest of the country it was $604, or nearly twice as much.

Even in "prosperous" 1929 southern farm people received an average gross income of only $186 a year as compared with $528 for farmers elsewhere. Out of that $186 southern farmers had to pay all their operating expenses — tools, fertilizer, seed, taxes, and interest on debt — so that only a fraction of that sum was left for the purchase of food, clothes, and the decencies of life. It is hardly surprising, therefore, that such ordinary items as automobiles, radios, and books are relatively rare in many southern country areas.

For more than half of the South's farm families — the 53 percent who are tenants without land of their own — incomes are far lower. Many thousands of them are living in poverty comparable to that of the poorest peasants in Europe. A recent study of southern cotton plantations indicated that the average tenant family received an income of only $73 per person for a year's work. Earnings of sharecroppers ranged from $38 to $87 per person, and an income of $38 annually means only a little more than 10 cents a day.

The South's industrial wages, like its farm income, are the lowest in the United States. In 1937 common labor in 20 important industries got 16 cents an hour less than laborers in other sections received for the same kind of work. Moreover, less than 10 percent of the textile workers are paid more than 52.5 cents an hour, while in the rest of the Nation 25 percent rise above this level. A recent survey of the South disclosed that the average annual wage in industry was only $865 while in the remaining States it averaged $1,219.

In income from dividends and interest the South is at a similar disadvantage. In 1937 the per capita income in the South from dividends and interest was only $17.55 as compared with $68.97 for the rest of the country.

Since the South's people live so close to the poverty line, its many local political subdivisions have had great difficulty in providing the schools and other public services necessary in any civilized community. In 1935 the assessed value of taxable property in the South averaged only $463 per person, while in the nine Northeastern States it amounted to $1,370. In other words, the Northeastern States had three times as much property per person to support their schools and other institutions.

Consequently, the South is not able to bring its schools and many other public services up to national standards, even though it tax the available wealth as heavily as any other section. In 1936 the State and local governments of the South collected only $28.88 per person while the States and local governments of the Nation as a whole collected $51.54 per person.

Although the South has 28 percent of the country's population, its Federal income-tax collections in 1934 were less than 12 percent of the national total. These collections averaged only $1.28 per capita throughout the South, ranging from 24 cents in Mississippi to $3.53 in Florida.

So much of the profit from southern industries goes to outside financiers, in the form of dividends and interest, that State income taxes would produce a meager yield in comparison with similar levies elsewhere. State taxation does not reach dividends which flow to corporation stockholders and management in other States; and, as a result, these people do not pay their share of the cost of southern schools and other institutions.

Under these circumstances the South has piled its tax burden on the backs of those least able to pay, in the form of sales taxes. (The poll tax[3] keeps the poorer citizens from voting in eight southern States; thus they have no effective means of protesting against sales taxes.) In every southern State but one, 59 percent of the revenue is raised by sales taxes. In the Northeast, on the other hand, not a single State gets more than 44 percent of its income from this source, and most of them get far less.

The efforts of southern communities to increase their revenues and to spread the tax burden more fairly have been impeded by the vigorous opposition of interests outside the region which control much of the South's wealth. Moreover, tax revision efforts have been hampered in some sections by the fear that their industries would move to neighboring communities which would tax them more lightly — or even grant them tax exemption for long periods.

The hope that industries would bring with them better living conditions and consequent higher tax revenues often has been defeated by the competitive tactics of the communities themselves. Many southern towns have found that industries which are not willing to pay their fair share of the cost of public services likewise are not willing to pay fair wages, and so add little to the community's wealth.

SECTION 6. EDUCATION

Great numbers of Americans are continually moving from one region to another. This makes poor schooling in any region a matter of national concern. Illiteracy, poor training, lack of education, go along with those migrating people who have not had schools. The fact that the South is the source of a considerable part of the rest of the Nation's population makes the South's difficulties in providing school facilities a national problem.

---

[3] The poll tax was a flat tax on individuals, or "polls." Poll taxes were widely used by southern states from the late nineteenth century into the 1960s. By requiring that such taxes be paid up cumulatively as a prerequisite to voting, states could prevent poorer citizens, primarily but not exclusively black, from voting. The Twenty-fourth Amendment to the U.S. Constitution (1964) prohibited the use of poll taxes to restrict voting in federal elections.

In the United States as a whole it is more possible than ever before to supply training for children and young people. The child population has only doubled since 1880, while the adult population has increased more than threefold. Too, the productive capacity per worker today is far in excess of what it was 50 years ago. In the South, however, owing to the higher birthrate and to the migration of adult workers, the proportion of productive workers to schoolchildren is much lower than elsewhere in the country. A study of this condition in 1930 showed that there were 10 adults to 6 children as compared to 10 adults for 4 children in the North and West.

In the rural regions of the South, particularly, there is a marked disparity between the number of children to be educated and the means for educating them. For example, in 1930 the rural inhabitants of the Southeast had to care for 4,250,000 children of school age of the country's total, although they received an income of only about 2 percent of the Nation's total. In the nonfarm population of the Northeast, on the other hand, there were 8,500,000 children in a group that received 42 percent of the total national income — 21 times as much income available to educate only twice as many children.

This disparity in the educational load, which bears so heavily on the South, continues. In 1936 the rate of natural increase in the population was greatest in the southeastern and southwestern sections of the United States, precisely where the lack of educational opportunity is already most pronounced.

The southern regions are affected by population shifts more than other sections because the greatest proportion of movers originate there. In the 1920's the States south of the Potomac and Ohio rivers and east of the Mississippi lost about 1,700,000 persons through migration, about half of whom were between 15 and 35 years of age. These persons moved at the beginning of their productive life to regions which got this manpower almost free of cost, whereas the South, which had borne the expense of their care and education up to the time when they could start producing, suffered an almost complete loss of its investment. The newcomers to the South did not, by any means, balance this loss. The cost of rearing and schooling the young people of the southern rural districts who moved to cities has been estimated to be approximately $250,000,000 annually.

The South must educate one-third of the Nation's children with one-sixth of the Nation's school revenues. According to the most conservative estimates, the per capita ability of the richest State in the country to support education is six times as great as that of the poorest State.

Although southern teachers compare favorably with teachers else where, the average annual salary of teachers in Arkansas for 1933 – 34 was $465, compared to $2,361 for New York State for the same year, and in no one of the Southern States was the average salary of teachers equal to the average of the Nation. In few places in the nation, on the other hand, is the number of pupils per teacher higher than as in the South. Overcrowding of schools, particularly in rural areas, has lowered the standards of education, and the short school terms of southern rural schools further reduce their effectiveness.

In the South only 16 percent of the children enrolled in school are in high school as compared with 24 percent in States outside the South.

Higher education in the South has lagged far behind the rest of the Nation. The total endowments of the colleges and universities of the South are less than the combined endowments of Yale and Harvard. As for medical schools, the South does not have the facilities to educate sufficient doctors for its own needs.

Since adequate schools and other means of public education are indispensable to the successful functioning of a democratic nation, the country as a whole is concerned with the South's difficulty in meeting its problem of education.

Illiteracy was higher in 1930 in the Southern States than in any other region, totaling 8.8 percent. The North Central States had a percentage of 1.9. New England and the Middle Atlantic States combined had a percentage of 3.5. In the South the percentages ranged from 2.8 in Oklahoma to 14.9 in South Carolina. Every State in the South except Oklahoma had a percentage higher than 6.5 percent.

But the poor educational status of the South is not a result of lack of effort to support schools. The South collects in total taxes about half as much per person as the Nation as a whole. All Southern States fall below the national average in tax resources per child, although they devote a larger share of their tax income to schools. For the Southern States to spend the national average per pupil would require an additional quarter of a billion dollars of revenue.

Between 1933 and 1935 more than $21,000,000 of Federal funds were necessary to keep rural schools open, and more than 80 percent of this amount was needed in the South, where local and State governments were unable to carry the burden.

In 1936 the Southern States spent an average of $25.11 per child in schools, or about half the average for the country as a whole, or a quarter of what was spent per child in New York State. In 1935 – 36 the average school child enrolled in Mississippi had $27.47 spent on his education. At the same time the average school child enrolled in New York State had

$141.43 spent on his education, or more than five times as much as was spent on a child in Mississippi. There were actually 1,500 school centers in Mississippi without school buildings, requiring children to attend school in lodge halls, abandoned tenant houses, country churches, and, in some instances, even in cotton pens.

SECTION 7. HEALTH

For years evidence has been piling up that food, clothing, and housing influence not only the sickness rate and death rate but even the height and weight of schoolchildren. In the South, where family incomes are exceptionally low, the sickness and death rates are unusually high. Wage differentials become in fact differentials in health and life; poor health, in turn, affects wages.

The low-income belt of the South is a belt of sickness, misery, and unnecessary death. Its large proportion of low-income citizens are more subject to disease than the people of any similar area. The climate cannot be blamed — the South is as healthful as any section for those who have the necessary care, diet, and freedom from occupational disease.

Several years ago the United States Public Health Service conducted syphilis-control demonstrations in selected rural areas in the South. These studies revealed a much higher ratio of syphilis among Negroes than among whites, but showed further that this higher ratio was not due to physical differences between the races. It was found to be due to the greater poverty and lower living conditions of the Negroes. Similar studies of such diseases have shown that individual health cannot be separated from the health of the community as a whole.

The presence of malaria, which infects annually more than 2,000,000 people, is estimated to have reduced the industrial output of the South one-third. One of the most striking examples of the effect of malaria on industry was revealed by the Public Health Service in studies among employees of a cotton mill in eastern North Carolina. Previous to the attempts to control malaria, the records of the mill one month showed 66 looms were idle as a result of ill-health. After completion of control work, no looms were idle for that reason. Before control work, 238,046 pounds of cloth were manufactured in one month. After completion of the work production rose to 316,804 pounds in one month — an increase of 33½ percent.

In reports obtained in 1935 from 9 lumber companies, owning 14 sawmill villages in 5 southern States, there was agreement that malaria was an important and increasing problem among the employees. During the year 7.6 percent of hospital admissions, 16.4 percent of physician calls, and 19.7 percent of dispensary drugs were for malaria. The average number of days off duty per case of malaria was 9, while days in the hospital for the same cause were 5. Ten railroads in the South listed malaria as an economic problem and a costly liability. Four utility companies had full-time mosquito-fighting crews at work during the year. The average case admitted to a company hospital lasted 3 days and the average number of days off duty because of malaria was 11. Each case of malaria was said to cost the companies $40.

If we attempt to place a monetary value on malaria by accepting the figure of $10,000 as the value of an average life and using the death rate of 3.943 for malaria reported by the census for 1936, the annual cost of deaths from this disease is $39,500,000. To this figure could be added the cost of illness, including days of work lost.

The health-protection facilities of the South are limited. For example, there are only one-third as many doctors per capita in South Carolina as there are in California. The South is deficient in hospitals and clinics, as well as in health workers. Many counties have no facilities at all.

The South has only begun to look into its pressing industrial hygiene problems, although it has 26 percent of the male mine workers in the United States and 14 percent of the male factory workers. These are the workers with which modern industrial health protection is most concerned.

The experience as to pneumonia and tuberculosis among employees of the Tennessee Coal, Iron & Railroad Co. and their dependents during the 11-year period from 1925 to 1935 gives an indication of health conditions among miners in the South. The situation generally is probably worse than shown by the figures for this company, whose workers have relatively better protection against disease. For this period the number under observation averaged slightly more than 77,000 persons. There were 3,780 cases of pneumonia, of which 739 terminated fatally. This resulted in an average frequency per 1,000 of approximately 4.9 pneumonia cases per year among surface workers, 4.7 among coal miners, and 10.6 among ore miners. The rate of 4.2 for dependents included also the pneumonia of childhood and infancy. A fatality rate of 30.7 deaths per 1,000 cases of pneumonia was found among surface workers, a rate of 26.8 among coal miners, and 24.8 among ore miners. Deaths from tuberculosis occurred at an annual rate of 1.467 per thousand workers among coal miners, 1.232 among ore miners, and 0.566 among surface workers.

Prior to 1936 only one State in the South gave consideration to industrial hygiene. Today, with the aid of Social Security funds, seven additional States have industrial-hygiene units, and approximately 7,000,000 of the 10,000,000 gainful workers are receiving some type of industrial-hygiene service. However, these industrial-hygiene units have started their programs only recently, and it will be some time before adequate health services will be available. The funds now being spent for this activity in the eight States which have industrial-hygiene services do not meet the problem of protecting and improving the health of these workers. Approximately $100,000 is now being budgeted for this work, although it is known that the economic loss due to industrial injuries and illnesses among these workers is hundreds of millions of dollars.

Reports of one of the largest life-insurance companies show that more people in the southern area than elsewhere die without medical aid. The same company reported in a recent year a rise of 7.3 percent in the death rate in the nine South Atlantic States, though in no other region had the death rate risen above 4.8 percent, and in some sections it had declined.

The scourge of pellagra,[4] that affects the South almost exclusively, is a disease chiefly due to inadequate diet; it responds to rather simple preventive measures, including suitable nourishing food. Even in southern cities from 60 to 88 percent of the families of low incomes are spending for food less than enough to purchase an adequate diet.

SECTION 8. HOUSING

The effects of bad housing can be measured directly in the general welfare. It lessens industrial efficiency, encourages inferior citizenship, lowers the standard of family life, and deprives people of reasonable comfort. There are also direct relationships between poor housing and poor health, and between poor housing and crime.

The type of slum most usual in southern towns consists of antiquated, poorly built rental quarters for working people. The rows of wooden houses without any modern improvements, without proper sanitary facilities, and often without running water, are usually in congested areas and in the least desirable locations. Often they are next to mills or mines where the tenants work, or on low swampy land subject to floods and no

---

[4] Pellagra, a debilitating disease caused by a deficiency of niacin (vitamin B_1) in the diet, was found to be endemic to the South in the early twentieth century. It especially afflicted the southern poor, whose corn-and-pork-based diet peculiarly lacked niacin and who often had to do without other foods.

good for anything else. They are usually far removed from playgrounds and other recreation areas. The southern slum has often been built to be a slum. It is simply a convenient barracks for a supply of cheap labor.

Lack of running water and impure water supplies are common in southern slums. Bathtubs, sinks, and laundry tubs are among the bare necessities that are often lacking in slum dwellings. Sometimes city water is supplied through a yard hydrant shared by several families. Surface wells are often contaminated on the farms and in the villages and small towns. Contaminated milk and contaminated water, frequently found, cause typhoid fever, which is becoming a widespread rural disease in the South.

Lack of sanitary flush toilets and sewer systems for waste disposal is characteristic not only of the great majority of farm and rural homes, but of a large proportion of homes in small towns and a substantial number in the cities. Twenty-six percent of southern city or town households are without indoor flush toilets as contrasted with 13.1 percent for the city and town households of the country as a whole. In extensive rural districts there are not only no indoor flush toilets, but no outdoor privies even of the most primitive sort. Nearly a fifth of all southern farm homes have no toilets at all. It is in these regions that hookworm infection and consequent anemia have flourished as a result of soil pollution.

There is also extensive overcrowding in the southern town areas. In one-eighth of the dwellings there are more than one and one-half persons per room. In the United States as a whole only one-fourteenth of town houses are so crowded. In 19 southern cities recently studied, over 40 percent of all dwellings rent for less than $15 a month or are valued at less than $1,500, as opposed to 24.6 percent for the 64 cities studied in the country as a whole. Only three of the southern cities had a smaller percentage of dilapidated houses than the national average. Five of the 8 cities with over a quarter of their houses in bad condition were in the South; 1 of these had 4 out of 10 of its houses either in need of repairs or unfit for habitation.

A study of blighted areas in New Orleans showed that their tuberculosis death rate was twice as high as the city's average, that their number of criminal arrests was 40 percent higher than the average, and that syphilis and cancer rates were high.

Houses in the rural South are the oldest, have the lowest value, and have the greatest need of repairs of any farmhouses in the United States.

That there are 2½ million below-standard houses would be a conservative estimate. Of 3 million farmhouses in 14 southern States, including West Virginia, surveyed in 1930 only 5.7 percent had water piped to the house and 3.4 percent had water piped to the bathroom. More than half the farmhouses are unpainted. More than a third of southern farmhouses do not have screens to keep out mosquitoes and flies.

If we consider below-standard all nonfarm dwellings in the 14 States renting for less than $10 a month, and all occupant-owned nonfarm dwellings valued at less than $1,500, we find 1½ million below-standard houses. Recent studies by local housing authorities in many of the southern cities indicate that these assumptions are correct. In addition, many houses now renting between $10 and $15 are definitely below standard. The average farmhouse in the South is worth about $650. The average farm renter's house is worth about $350, according to the Federal census of 1930.

Southern cities have one important advantage over northern cities in their approach to the housing problem. As a rule, they are not hampered by the excessive land valuations that have developed in the North with the rapid growth and centralization of industry. Although the 1930 census shows that the rate of movement to cities and towns is greater in the South than in the North, the effect of this is not yet reflected in town and city land values and is not likely to be while wages remain low. It is, however, reflected in poorer living conditions, overcrowding, and greater danger of the spread of certain diseases.

By the most conservative estimates, 4,000,000 southern families should be rehoused. This is one-half of all families in the South.

SECTION 9. LABOR

The rapidly growing population of the South is faced with the problem of finding work that will provide a decent living. Neither on the farm nor in the factory is there the certainty of a continuing livelihood, and thousands of southerners shift each year from farm to mill or mine and back again to farm.

The insecurity of work in southern agriculture, its changes in method, and its changes in location, make the labor problem of the South not simply an industrial labor problem. Neither the farm population nor the industrial workers can be treated separately, because both groups, as a whole, receive too little income to enable their members to accumulate the property that tends to keep people stable. Industrial labor in the South is to a great extent unskilled and, therefore, subject to the competition of recurring migrations from the farm — people who have lost in the gamble of one-crop share farming. On the other hand, the industrial workers, with low wages and long hours, are constantly tempted to return to the farm for another try.

As industries requiring a large proportion of skilled workers have been slow in developing, the unskilled industrial labor in the South is particularly hampered by the competition of unskilled workers from the farms who accept low wages in preference to destitution at home. Much of the South's increase in industrial activity has been brought about by the removal of cotton goods manufacturing plants to the Southeast from higher wage areas in New England. This backbone of southern industry ranks nationally as one of the low-wage manufacturing industries. In the South it pays even lower wages than elsewhere. According to 1937 figures, the pay for the most skilled work in this industry is about 12 cents an hour less in the South than the pay for the same work elsewhere. The figures for the cotton goods industry also show the large number of low-wage workers and the small number receiving high wages in the South. More than half of the workers in southern mills earn under 37.5 cents an hour, although in the rest of the country the industry employs less than 10 percent at such low rates. In the South less than one-tenth of the workers are paid more than 52.5 cents an hour, although one-fourth of the workers in the rest of the Nation's cotton goods industry are paid above this rate.

Similar differentials between the South and other regions are found in lumber, furniture, iron and steel, coal mining, and other industries generally. The influence of the farm population's competition is shown in the unskilled occupations where these wage differentials are widest. The average differential in rates for new labor between the South and the rest of the country in 20 of the country's important industries in 1937 amounted to 16 cents an hour.

In spite of longer working hours, the total annual wages show the same discrepancy. The average yearly pay per person in industry and business in the South in 1935 was $865.41 as compared with $1,219.31 for the rest of the country.

Wage differentials are reflected in lower living standards. Differences in costs of living between the southern cities and cities in the Nation as a whole are not great enough to justify the differentials in wages that exist. In 1935 a study of costs of living showed that a minimum emergency standard required a family income of $75.27 a month as an average for all the cities surveyed. The average of costs in southern cities showed that $71.94 a month would furnish the minimum emergency standard. This would indicate a difference of less than 5 percent in living costs. Industrial earnings for workers are often 30 to 50 percent below national averages.

Low wages and poverty are in great measure self-perpetuating. Labor organization has made slow and difficult progress among the low-paid workers, and they have had little collective bargaining power or organized influence on social legislation. Tax resources have been low because of low incomes in the communities, and they have been inadequate to provide for the type of education modern industry requires. Malnutrition has had its influence on the efficiency of workers. Low living standards have forced other members of workers' families to seek employment to make ends meet. These additions to the labor market tend further to depress wages.

Low wages have helped industry little in the South. Not only have they curtailed the purchasing power on which local industry is dependent, but they have made possible the occasional survival of inefficient concerns. The standard of wages fixed by such plants and by agriculture has lowered the levels of unskilled and semiskilled workers, even in modern and well-managed establishments. While southern workers, when well trained and working under modern conditions, are thoroughly efficient producers, there is not enough such employment to bring the wage levels into line with the skill of the workers.

Unemployment in the South has not resulted simply from the depression. Both in agriculture and industry, large numbers have for years been living only half-employed or a quarter employed or scarcely employed at all. In the problem of unemployment in the South, the relation between agriculture and industry becomes notably clear. Over 30 percent of the persons employed on emergency works programs are farmers and farm laborers, as compared to 15.3 percent for the country as a whole. The insecurity of southern farmers is reflected in these figures. Seasonal wages in agriculture do not provide incomes sufficient to tide workers over the slack seasons. Part-time industrial work does not provide security the year round. As long as the agricultural worker cannot gain assurance of a continuing existence on the farm, he remains a threat to the job, the wages, and the working conditions of the industrial worker.

SECTION 10. WOMEN AND CHILDREN

Child labor is more common in the South than in any other section of the Nation, and several Southern States are among those which have the largest proportion of their women in gainful work. Moreover, women and children work under fewer legal safeguards than women and children elsewhere in the Nation.

Low industrial wages for men in the South frequently force upon their children as well as their wives a large part of the burden of family support. In agriculture, because of poor land and equipment, entire families must work in order to make their living.

The 1930 census, latest source of comprehensive information on child labor, showed that about three-fourths of all gainfully employed children from 10 to 15 years old worked in the Southern States, although these States contained less than one-third of the country's children between those ages.

Child labor, itself due to low wages for adult workers, is also a source of cheap competing labor, and thus it tends to make wages even lower, hours even longer, and generally to break down labor standards. Child labor, therefore, affects not only the child itself, but it undermines security of adult workers, and thus reacts seriously on the whole community and, indeed, the whole Nation.

The South leads the Nation in the employment of children in both farm and industrial work. One hundred eight out of every 1,000 children between 10 and 15 years old were employed in the South, compared to 47 out of every 1,000 children of these ages in the country as a whole. Only Oklahoma and Virginia, of all the Southern States, employ fewer child workers than the average for the country. Child labor legislation in these 13 States, as in the United States in general, does not apply to agricultural work, but is directed primarily to industrial and commercial employment. In some instances the coverage of the law is restricted to a few types of industrial establishments, and in other instances the laws themselves contain exemptions which greatly weaken their effectiveness. Only North and South Carolina have established a basic minimum age of 16 years for employment. Texas has a 15-year minimum age standard, but it applies only to factory and related employment. The remaining 10 States have a minimum age of 14, but in 8 of the 10 States the laws contain exemptions permitting employment below this age.

The effectiveness of child labor legislation depends upon the provisions for its enforcement. Employment certification and proper inspection are necessary to make such legislation effective. Three of the five States in the country which have not made legal provision for employment certificates are Southern States.

Employment of children affects school attendance. The proportion of children 10 to 15 years of age in the Southern States attending school in 1930 was 90 percent, as compared with 94 percent for the United States as a whole. If consideration were given to the number of days of school attendance, the disparity would appear much greater; the school term generally is shorter in the South than in other sections.

The upper age for compulsory school attendance throughout the rest of the country is generally 16 to 18. However, two Southern States require attendance only to 14, one to 15, and only in two States does the upper age extend above 16 years. All permit exemptions which materially lessen their effectiveness.

In many parts of the South legislation to protect women workers and to establish proper working standards for them has not been well developed. This has had far-reaching effects on the health, the living conditions, and the general well-being of women and their families.

In a region where workers generally are exploited, women are subjected to an even more intense form of exploitation. Many women work more than 50 hours a week in cotton and other textile mills, and in the shoe, bag, paper box, drug, and similar factories in certain Southern States.

The South has two of the four states in the entire Nation that have enacted no laws whatever to fix maximum hours for women workers. Only one of the Southern States has established an 8-hour day for women in any industry. Only four of the Southern States have applied a week as short as 48 hours for women in any industry.

Reports for a number of industries, including cotton manufacturing, have shown wage earners receiving wages well below those estimated by the Works Progress Administration as the lowest which would maintain a worker's family.

Women's wages ordinarily amount to less than men's. However, only two of the Southern States have enacted a law providing a minimum wage for women, though several others are attempting to pass such legislation. Recent payroll figures show women textile workers in an important southern textile State receiving average wages 10 percent below the average outside the South. Other figures show that a week's wage of less than $10 was received by more than half the women in one State's cotton mills, and by a large part of the women in the seamless hosiery plants of three States and in the men's work-clothes factories of two States.

Many women, even though employed full time, must receive public aid because their wages are insufficient to care for themselves and their children. The community thus carries part of the burden of these low wages and, in effect, subsidizes the employer.

One condition tending to lower women's wages is the system by which factories "farm out" work to be done in homes. Women have been found at extremely low pay doing such work as making artificial flowers, sewing buttons on cards, clocking hosiery, embroidering children's clothing, stuffing and stitching baseballs. Although this is a relatively recent tendency in the South, there are indications that such work is increasing. Usually the pay is far below that paid in the factory. A study of industrial home work on infants' wear disclosed that the women worked much longer hours than in the factory, though half of them received less than $2.73 for their week's work.

A low wage scale means low living standards, insufficient food for many, a great amount of illness, and, in general, unhealthful and undesirable conditions of life.

SECTION 11. OWNERSHIP AND USE OF LAND

The farming South depends on cotton and tobacco for two-thirds of its cash income. More than half of its farmers depend on cotton alone. They are one-crop farmers, subjected year after year to risks which would appall the average businessman. All their eggs are in one basket — a basket which can be upset, and often is, by the weather, the boll weevil,[5] or the cotton market.

The boll weevil can be conquered, and weather hazards tend to cancel themselves out as good seasons follow bad; but the cotton market is a sheer gamble. On this gamble nearly 2,000,000 southern families stake their year's work and everything they own. Their only chance of making a living is tied up with the fluctuations of the world price of cotton.

No other similar area in the world gambles its welfare and the destinies of so many people on a single crop market year after year.

The gamble is not a good one. Few other crops are subject to such violent and unpredictable price variations as cotton. In 1927 cotton farmers got 20 cents a pound for their crop; in 1929 they got 16 cents; in 1931 they got 6 cents; in 1933 they got 10 cents. Only once during the last decade did the price of cotton change less than 10 percent between pickings. Three times in 5 years it jumped more than 40 percent — once up and twice down.

Because cotton is the cornerstone of the economy of many parts of the South, the merchants, manufacturers, businessmen, and bankers share the hazards of the farmer. The men who finance cotton farming

---

[5] The boll weevil, an insect pest that attacked cotton bolls before they ripened, sharply reducing crop yields, entered the United States from Mexico in the 1890s and blanketed the Cotton Belt by the 1920s. While control measures were quickly developed, its appearance added greatly to the cost, labor, and risk of southern farming, and contributed materially to southern poverty.

charge high interest rates because their money is subject to far more than the normal commercial risk. As a result, the mortgage debt of southern farm owners has been growing steadily for the last 20 years. A check-up on 46 scattered counties in the South in 1934 showed that one-tenth of the farm land was in the hands of corporations, mostly banks and insurance companies, which had been forced to foreclose their mortgages.

This process has forced more than half of the South's farmers into the status of tenants, tilling land they do not own. Whites and Negroes have suffered alike. Of the 1,831,000 tenant families in the region, about 66 percent are white. Approximately half of the sharecroppers are white, living under economic conditions almost identical with those of Negro sharecroppers.

The pattern of southern tenancy was set at the end of the War between the States, which left thousands of former slave owners with plenty of land but no capital or labor to work it. Hundreds of thousands of former slaves and impoverished whites were willing to work but had no land. The result was the crop-sharing system, under which the land was worked by men who paid for the privilege with a share of their harvest. It was natural under this system that landowners should prefer to have virtually all the land put in cotton or other cash crops from which they could easily get their money. Consequently, over wide areas of the South cash-cropping, one-crop farming, and tenant farming have come to mean practically the same thing. Diversification has been difficult, because the landlord and tenant usually have not been able to find a workable method of financing, producing, and sharing the return from such crops as garden truck, pigs, and dairy products.

Tenant families form the most unstable part of our population. More than a third of them move every year, and only a small percentage stay on the same place long enough to carry out a 5-year crop rotation. Such frequent moves are primarily the result of the traditional tenure system, under which most renters hold the land by a mere spoken agreement, with no assurance that they will be on the same place next season. Less than 2 percent have written leases which give them security of tenure for more than one year.

Under these circumstances the tenant has no incentive to protect the soil, plant cover crops, or keep buildings in repair. On the contrary, he has every reason to mine the soil for every possible penny of immediate cash return.

The moving habit, moreover, is costly. Most renters merely swap farms every few years without gain to themselves or anybody else. The bare cost of moving has been estimated at about $57 per family, or more than $25,000,000 annually for the tenants of the South. Children are taken out of school in midyear, and usually fall behind with their studies. It is almost impossible for a family constantly on the move to take an active part in community affairs; and, as a consequence, churches and other institutions suffer. For example, in one area of North Carolina where the percentage of tenancy is low, there were 257 churches, with 21,000 members. In a nearby area of high tenancy — with three and one-half times as many people — there were only 218 churches, with 17,000 members.

While it is growing more cotton and tobacco than it can use or sell profitably, the South is failing to raise the things it needs. Southern farmers grow at home less than one-fifth of the things they use; four-fifths of all they eat and wear is purchased.

For example, the region has more than half of the Nation's farm people, yet it raises less than one-third of the Nation's pigs and cattle. Although it has more than a fourth of America's total population, it produces only one-fifth of the country's eggs, milk, and butter, one-seventh of the hay, one-eighth of the potatoes, and one-twelfth of the oats. Consequently the South must either obtain these things from other regions and pay handling and freight charges or do without.

Too many southern families have simply done without, and as a result they have suffered severely from malnutrition and dietary diseases. Many common vegetables are rarities in many southern farming communities, although both soil and climate are extremely favorable to their growth. Production of foodstuffs could be increased manyfold in the South without infringing on the markets of any other region; most of the increased output could, and should, be absorbed by the very farm families producing it.

Because they have concentrated on cash crops, southern farmers have planted relatively little of their land in alfalfa, clover, field peas, and soybeans. These and similar legumes add fertility to the soil and at the same time protect fields against washing and gullying. If widely used, they would help the farmer to protect his investment in his land and take a little of the gamble out of his business.

On the other hand, cotton, tobacco, and corn use up the natural richness of the land with great speed. Fields planted to them year after year wear out and wash away much more quickly than fields on which legumes are planted in rotation with cash crops. Yet 6 acres of southern crop land out of every 10 are planted one season after another in cotton, tobacco, and corn.

SECTION 12. CREDIT

There has never been enough capital and credit in the South to meet the needs of its farmers and its industry. Its people have been living so close to poverty that the South has found it almost impossible to scrape together enough capital to develop its natural resources for the benefit of its own citizens.

Lacking capital of its own, the South has been forced to borrow from outside financiers, who have reaped a rich harvest in the form of interest and dividends. At the same time it has had to hand over the control of much of its business and industry to investors from wealthier sections.

A glance at the bank reports shows how difficult it has been for the southern people, whose average income is the lowest in the Nation, to build up savings of their own. Although the region contains 28 percent of the country's population, in July 1937, its banks held less than 11 percent of the Nation's bank deposits, or only $150 per capita, as compared with $471 per capita for the rest of the United States. Savings deposits were less than 6 percent of the national total. Of the 66 banks having deposits of $100,000,000 or more only two are in the South, and they barely qualify.

Even these figures do not fully disclose how small a share the South plays in the country's financial life. Southern investment banking firms managed only 0.07 percent of the security issues larger than $1,000,000 which were offered for sale between July 1, 1936, and June 1, 1938 — and it is the investment bankers who find the money for virtually all important industries.

Insurance company funds reflect the same story. Southern companies hold only $756,000,000, or about 2.6 percent, of the $28,418,000,000 of assets held by the Nation's life-insurance companies.

The scarcity of local credit sources results in high interest rates and lays a heavy burden both on individuals and local governments. The average interest paid on southern State, county, and municipal bonds is 4.4 percent, while the rest of the country pays only 3.98. The weighted average interest rates charged by banks in 27 large southern and western cities in June 1938 was 4.14 percent, while for New York City it was only 2.36 percent, and for 8 other northern and eastern cities only 3.38 percent.

State banks outside the Federal Reserve System, but insured by the Federal Deposit Insurance Corporation, charge average interest rates in the South ranging from 6.5 percent in Virginia to 10.43 percent in Texas and 11.5 percent in Oklahoma. In the New England and the Middle Atlantic States, on the other hand, it is 5.75 percent. In the Mountain

States the highest average is 8.5 percent, which is lower than in 5 of the Southern States.

Banking laws and regulations have contributed still further to the scarcity of southern credit. Ordinarily, banks can make credit available for capital purposes only by the purchase of readily marketable securities. This makes it almost necessary for a security to be listed on an exchange or to have an active over-the-counter market. Locally owned southern industries are usually too small to meet these requirements. Recently these requirements have been liberalized, but it is too early to tell whether the change will be helpful.

Faced with these handicaps, the South has had to look beyond its boundaries for the financing of virtually all of its large industries and many of its small ones. This has turned policy-making powers over to outside managements whose other interests often lead them to exercise their authority against the South's best advantage. For example, many such companies buy most of their goods outside of the South, and often their sales policies are dictated in the interest of allied corporations in other sections of the country.

If the high cost of credit has hampered southern industry, its effect on farming might be illustrated by the remark of Louis XIV: "Credit supports agriculture, as the rope supports the hanged." Almost the only sources of credit for small farmers — aside from Federal agencies — are (1) local banks, (2) landlords, and (3) merchants and dealers.

The banks cannot meet all credit demands, because whatever scant deposits they may have are largest in the fall and winter, after harvest, and smallest in the spring and summer, when the need for farm financing is greatest.

As a result, the majority of southern tenant farmers must depend for credit on their landlords or the "furnish merchant" who supplies seed, food, and fertilizer. Their advances, in fact, have largely replaced currency for a considerable part of the rural population. For security the landlord or merchant takes a lien on the entire crop, which is to be turned over to him immediately after harvest in settlement of the debt. Usually he keeps the books and fixes the interest rate. Even if he is fair and does not charge excessive interest, the tenants often find themselves in debt at the end of the year. This is not necessarily a reflection on the planter-merchant; very often he would like to improve the lot of his tenants but must exploit them in order that he himself may survive.

The credit difficulties of the landlord are only a little less oppressive than those of his tenants. Because he ordinarily stakes everything on a single cash crop — cotton or tobacco — which is subject to wildly fluctuating markets, the landowner is a poor credit risk. Consequently he often must pay interest rates as high as 20 percent, making the rates for tenants range considerably higher.

Attempts to find a remedy through credit unions have met with slight success, although such organizations are spreading. On January 1, 1938, there were 564 Federal credit unions in the South, with 80,530 members and assets totaling $2,851,500. The unions are not evenly distributed throughout the region, however, since Texas alone had 167 while Kentucky had only 4.

Some of the South's credit difficulties have been slightly relieved in recent years by the extension of credit from Federal agencies — to the businessman by the Reconstruction Finance Corporation, to the farmer by the Farm Security and Farm Credit Administrations, to municipalities by the Public Works Administration. Many other agencies, ranging from the Works Progress Administration to the Soil Conservation Service, have brought desperately needed funds into the South.

The fact remains, however, that the South has not yet been able to build up an adequate supply of credit — the basis of the present-day economic system.

SECTION 13. USE OF NATURAL RESOURCES

The great natural resources of the South have been exploited with the traditional American regard for cream and disregard for skimmed milk. Perhaps no worse than in the rest of the country, but with serious effect on the South, forests have been girdled, chopped, and burned without regard for their permanent value as timber or as conservers of the soil and rainfall.

Ruthless measures have been used to obtain the best ore, oil, or gas with the least effort. Careless room-and-pillar [6] mining has resulted in the abandonment of untold tons of southern coal in deserted mines. In 1935 the Nation lost through wastage 479,826,000,000 cubic feet of natural gas, not including wastage at the wellheads. The Panhandle section of Texas alone accounted for 67 percent of this extravagant loss. Other sections of the South, similarly guilty, failed to take advantage of inventions which would have saved and used much of their gas.

---

[6] "Room and pillar" mining for coal sought to save the cost of constructing mine tunnels by leaving pillars of coal to support the roofs of tunnels and underground rooms. When the remaining coal was depleted and the mine abandoned, the pillars would be abandoned as well, a practice the authors of the *Report* regarded as "wasteful."

Because of the poverty in which the South was left after the War between the States, and because of the high cost of credit since that time, a very large share of the natural resources of the South is owned in other regions. To the extent that this is true, the South is exposed to a double danger. On the one hand, it is possible for a monopolistic corporation in another region of the country to purchase and leave unused resources in the South which otherwise might be developed in competition with the monopoly. On the other hand, the large absentee ownership of the South's natural resources and the South's industry makes it possible for residents elsewhere to influence greatly the manner in which the South is developed and to subordinate that development to other interests outside the South.

The public utilities in the South are almost completely controlled by outside interests. All the major railroad systems are owned and controlled elsewhere. Most of the great electric holding company systems, whose operating companies furnish the light, heat, and power for southern homes and industries, are directed, managed, and owned by outside interests. Likewise, the transmission and distribution of natural gas, one of the South's great assets, is almost completely in the hands of remote financial institutions. The richest deposits of the iron ore, coal, and limestone that form the basis for the steel industry in Birmingham are owned or controlled outside of the region. Until recently, too, the Birmingham area was subordinated to the Pittsburgh area as a result of a system of pricing steel which placed it at a tremendous disadvantage. As a result of this disadvantage — that is, because it was more economical for them to be in the areas formerly favored by the artificial price system — the fabrication plants which use most of the steel were not constructed in the Birmingham area. The fact that these fabrication plants are outside of the South will make it hard for the South now to find a ready market for its steel, even though the pricing system has been changed.

Most of the rich deposits of bauxite, from which aluminum is made, are owned or controlled outside the region. Practically all important deposits of zinc ore in the South are owned elsewhere, and the principal zinc-mining company in the Southwest is a subsidiary of a company completely owned and controlled outside of the area of its operation. The South's resources of zinc ore and the South's consumption of zinc paints and metalware are separated by a long northern detour, because absentee ownership and discriminatory freight rates make it cheaper to ship raw materials north for processing than to manufacture them at home.

Over 99 percent of the sulfur produced in the United States comes from Texas and Louisiana. Two extraction companies control practically the entire output. Both are owned and controlled outside the South. One has 15 directors and the other 9, but only 1 member of each board resides in the South.

For mining its mineral wealth and shipping it away in a raw or semifinished form the South frequently receives nothing but the low wages of unskilled and semiskilled labor. The wages for manufacturing this natural wealth into finished products often do not go to southerners, but to workers in other areas; and the profits likewise usually go to financial institutions in other regions. When a southerner buys the finished product, on the other hand, the price he pays includes all the wasteful cross-hauling involved in the present system.

In North Carolina and Tennessee is produced 36 percent of the total ground feldspar of the Nation; but one can look in vain in the South for any important tile, glass, enamel, insulator, or scouring soap industries using this product. Georgia produces 66 percent of the kaolin output of the country and South Carolina 20 percent; but their industries use little of this clay. Kentucky is a ranking fluorspar producer, but practically its entire production is shipped out of the South. The processing of cotton into textiles is the major southern industry; but many of the largest mills are owned outside of the region. Other mills are only recent emigrants from northern locations to the South.

The manufacture of cellulose into artificial silk, or rayon, presents a striking example of absentee ownership. The American Bemberg Corporation, with large mills in Tennessee, uses patents and processes exclusively owned in Germany. Of the company's 14 directors, 5 are German, 3 are Dutch, and 4 are American residents in New York.

SECTION 14. INDUSTRY

Since the War between the States industry has become in the minds of most Americans a symbol of profit and wealth. Certainly the wealthiest parts of our country are the most industrialized. There has long been a strong "New South" movement striving to achieve for the South the wealth that is supposed to come from industry.

With respect to the manufacture of cotton textiles, the South has come from a subordinate position in 1860 to a dominating position today. It is natural that the South's most outstanding accomplishment in industry should be the processing of its greatest agricultural crop. The cotton manufacturing industry started in the latter part of the nineteenth century with small subscriptions of stock provided, for the most part, by southerners; but when these mills began to compete successfully with the New England mills northern capital was introduced, and later a great many northern mills were shifted to the South.

Earnings on the investment in the southern mills, as indicated by figures for 1933 – 34, are considerably higher than those in the North, but the wages paid as reported from 1919 to 1933 are considerably less.

During the year 1933 the percentage of the wages to the value added by manufacture was 60.8 percent in five States in New England, as against 55.5 percent in five Southern States.

The development in recent years of the manufacture of cottonseed products has proved valuable to the South. In 1929 the value of these products reached $265,247,000, about half of which was for cottonseed oil. The further development of cottonseed oil for oleomargarine and kindred products has been hampered by taxes, licenses, and other restrictive legislation not only by States outside the region but also by the Federal Government.

The manufacture of cigarettes has become important in North Carolina and Virginia. The iron and coal industries are important in Alabama. The use of the southern forests for many purposes has constantly grown. In January 1938 the South had 38 pulp mills built or being built, with a total investment estimated at some $200,000,000. Many new uses have been found for this pulp, such as the manufacture of building boards, rayon staple fiber, wrapping paper, and quite recently newsprint paper. As the United States is the largest consumer of wood pulp in the world, the development of this industry in the South is significant.

Meager facilities exist in the South for research that might lead to the development of new industries especially adapted to the South's resources. Some new industries have been developing in the South, but others have disappeared.

In addition to absentee ownership and the high cost of credit, the major problem which faces almost all industry in the South is that of freight rate differentials. The present interterritorial freight rates which apply on movements into other areas of many southern manufactured and semi-finished goods, and some agricultural products and raw materials, handicap the development of industry in the south. This disadvantage works a hardship particularly with regard to shipments into the important northeastern territory. This region, containing 51 percent of the Nation's population, is the greatest consuming area. The southeastern manufacturer sending goods across the boundary into this region is at a relative disadvantage of approximately 39 percent in the charges which he has to pay as compared with the rates for similar shipments entirely within the eastern rate territory. The southwestern manufacturer, with a 75 percent relative disadvantage, is even worse off. Such a disadvantage applies to the southern shipper even when, distance considered, he is entirely justified on economic grounds in competing with producers within the eastern territory.

In effect, this difference in freight rates creates a man-made wall to replace the natural barrier long since overcome by modern railroad engineering. Both actual and potential southern manufacturers are hampered because attractive markets are restricted by the existence of a barrier that is now completely artificial. The southern producer, attempting to build up a large-scale production on the decreasing cost principle, finds his goods barred from the wider markets in the Nation's most populous area. In marketing his products over the wall he is forced to absorb the differences in freight charges.

Two chief reasons for higher freight rates have disappeared. One was the greater expense of railroading in the South, due to physical difficulties. This has been minimized by modern engineering. Another was the comparative lack of traffic that prevented the spreading of the cost. This no longer is the case, since many important southern roads have as great a traffic density as those above the Ohio River. The operating costs of southern lines today are lower than those in the eastern territory.

The artificial rate structure handicaps the South in its efforts to expand and diversify its industry. For example, under present conditions it is cheaper to concentrate and ship the South's zinc ore to the North, where it is made into metallic zinc, used to coat northern steel, and shipped back to the South for its "tin" roofs and other galvanized ironware, than it is to convert this zinc ore in the South without the economic loss of cross hauling.

An equally serious deterrent to the South's economic development has been the Nation's traditional high tariff policy. The South has been forced for generations to sell its agricultural products in an unprotected world market, and to buy its manufactured goods at prices supported by high tariffs. The South, in fact, has been caught in a vise that has kept it from moving along with the mainstream of American economic life. On the one hand, the freight rates have hampered its industry; on the other hand, our high tariff has subsidized industry in other sections of the country at the expense of the South. Penalized for being rural, and handicapped in its efforts to industrialize, the economic life of the South has been squeezed to a point where the purchasing power of the southern people does not provide an adequate market for its own industries nor an attractive market for those of the rest of the country.

Moreover, by curtailing imports, the tariff has reduced the ability of foreign countries to buy American cotton and other agricultural exports. America's trade restrictions, without sufficient expansion of our domestic markets for southern products, have hurt the South more than any other region.

SECTION 15. PURCHASING POWER

The South is the Nation's greatest untapped market and the market in which American business can expand most easily. The cost of "selling" the South modern conveniences is already being borne, to large extent, since the methods that now sell the rest of the Nation reach the South with little or no extra cost. Radio, movies, periodicals, and other instruments of national scope for acquainting the public with new things have "sold" southerners as they have sold other Americans. There are no language barriers, no geographical obstacles, no tariff walls, no psychological difficulties to be overcome. The people of the South need to buy, they want to buy, and they would buy — if they had the money.

The South has an abundance of the things the Nation needs. Its vast stores of raw materials — forest, mineral, and agricultural; its extensive power resources — water, coal, oil, and natural gas; its ample transportation facilities — rail, water, and air — and its varied climate, could make the South a tremendous trader with the rest of the Nation. Its growing population, with vast needs and desires, now largely unfilled, could keep a large part of the rest of the country busy supplying them. Such a relationship would help the South and the rest of the Nation. Both have lost because this relationship does not exist.

The South's people want and need houses, radios, butter, beef, vegetables, milk, eggs, dresses, shirts, shoes. They want and could use the many thousands of things, little and big, that men and machines make to bring health and good living to people. The average southerner with a total income of $315 could spend, without help, twice that amount for the things he needs and needs badly.

A study of southern farm-operating white families not receiving relief or other assistance showed that those whose income averaged $390 spent annually only $49 on the food they bought, $31 on clothing, $12 on medical care, $1 on recreation, $1 on reading, $2 on education. A similar study of southern white village residents showed that those whose incomes were under $750 a year spent 75 cents or more out of every dollar for food, clothing, housing, heating, lighting, and running the house. Only one in four of these families owned an automobile of any description.

Southern people need food. The all too common diet in the rural South of fatback, corn bread, and molasses, with its resulting pellagra and other dietary diseases, is not dictated by taste alone. There is a deficiency in the consumption of necessary foods even among employed, wage-earning families in the cities of the South. The average per capita butter consumption in cities in this region was found to be about half of that in eastern cities and a quarter of that in cities on the Pacific coast. Studies of gainfully employed nonrelief white workers in ten of the largest cities of the South showed that less than two-thirds spent enough money to buy an "adequate diet at minimum cost," as calculated by the Bureau of Home Economics. This same study gives further evidence of underconsumption by wage earners and lower salaried clerical workers. No relief families were studied.

The fact that the families who could spend annually $500 or over per person consumed well over half again as much meat, poultry, fish, and eggs, about four times as much cheese, twice as many tomatoes, 30 percent more bread, and well over twice as much fruit of all kinds as the families who could spend $300 annually per person reveals the possibility of a vastly increased market for foodstuffs of all kinds. The extent of the South's underconsumption of these basic foodstuffs can be estimated from the fact that half of the people of the South have an income of less than $300 a year.

Southern people need clothes. Farm families in Mississippi and Georgia with annual incomes below $250 spent between $19 and $41 for clothing per year. In villages husband-and-wife families not on relief, with incomes of less than $500 a year, spent $14 for the husband's and $15 for the wife's clothing; of these amounts, they spent $3 for shoes and shoe repairs, $1 for coats and other wraps, $1 for hats and caps. Farm families having similar incomes spent $15 for the husband's wardrobe, $12 for the wife's.

One-half of the southern people, and an even larger percent of rural southerners, need new houses. More than 90 percent of the rural families need water piped into their houses; even more need water in their bathrooms; over one-half of their houses need paint, one-third of them need screen on their windows, one-fifth do not even have privies. More than a fourth of the urban households need toilets, many of them need more bedrooms, over one-fifth of the houses are in need of repainting.

Of white nonrelief families in four southern cities with incomes less than $500, over one-third had no indoor running water, almost one-half had no kitchen sink with drain, none had gas or electricity for cooking, none had central heating. Among southern farm families of the same income group, less than 1 percent had an indoor water supply, less than 3 percent had kitchen sinks with drains, 1 percent had indoor toilets, none had electric or gas cooking facilities, and less than 2 percent electric lights.

They need these improvements and they need household equipment. In 33 villages in the Southeast recently surveyed, a smaller percentage of families owned washing, ironing, and sewing machines and vacuum cleaners than families in any of the four other regions studied. Only 2 percent of the white families and 0.3 percent of the Negro families of these southern villages owned washing machines, as compared with 81.2 percent in the Pennsylvania, Ohio, Michigan, Wisconsin, and Illinois villages that were surveyed, and 77.3 percent in a similar group of California, Oregon, and Washington villages. While about the same proportion of southern white villagers had refrigerators as New Englanders, only half as many southern Negro villagers were as fortunate. There was an even greater disparity in these household equipment items between southern farm families and farmers elsewhere in the country. And southern farmers need equipment. They need implements, fencing, and fertilizer.

Northern producers and distributors are losing profits and northern workers are losing work because the South cannot afford to buy their goods.

PART THREE

Related Pictures,
Life Stories, Statistics,
and Documents

Facing page
Figure 1. Southern Farm Technology: Cotton Chopping, Clarendon County, South Carolina, 1939

Next left
Figure 2. Southern Farm Technology: Cotton Picking, Pulaski County, Arkansas, 1935

Second right
Figure 3. Rural White Women at Home: Orange County, North Carolina, 1939

Second left
Figure 4. Southern Education: School, Skyline Farms, Alabama, 1937

Figure 5. Organized Labor Looks at "Runaway Shops": Cartoon on
the Cover of Thomas L. Stokes's *Carpetbaggers of Industry*

Personal: Life Stories from the Depression-Era South

In order to understand the concerns of the *Report*'s authors, it will be helpful to look at conditions in the South of the 1930s through the eyes of contemporaries. The documents in this chapter are personal accounts from some of those most affected by southern poverty. These accounts have been drawn from a remarkable collection of interviews conducted during the later 1930s by unemployed writers receiving work relief from the Works Progress Administration (WPA), and illustrate the privations, the daily struggles, and the social and political observations of poor southerners, white and black, tenant farmer and industrial worker. As you read, consider how the basic life concerns of these southerners relate to the themes of the *Report*.

MARY A. HICKS AND
WILLIS S. HARRISON

"You're Gonna Have Lace Curtains":
A White Tenant Family, North Carolina

John and Sarah Easton, with their sixteen-year-old twin girls, live in a one-room filling station near Wilson. It was once painted white but now is a weather-beaten gray. The top bricks have fallen from the jaunty flue and the tin roof shows numerous patches here and there. The steps sag and the whole place looks neglected but clean. In the yard is clean bare sand, but over on one side is a weed-grown flower bed.

"You're Gonna Have Lace Curtains," in Federal Writer's Project, *These Are Our Lives* (Chapel Hill: University of North Carolina Press, 1939), 3 – 17.

"Oh, you brought Amy home," said Sarah, as she stood in the door. Then she added, "Do come in, I'm not ashamed of our house although it's the worst we've stayed in since we was married thirty-two years ago. The main thing is that we hope to do better after next year."

She is a pleasant-voiced woman, big and strong with the brownest eyes one can imagine. Her hair is heavily streaked with gray and there are many tired lines in her dark face. Her mouth has bitter lines as though she long ago screwed it the wrong way when she was inclined to laugh.

"The children are all low like their father except Jack. He is tall and rawboned like I was when I was young." She looked down at her plump figure. "I reckon they'll all be fat, though, when they git older like me and their father. Do have a chair. Have you ever seen such a change in the weather a day after Thanksgiving in your life? I do believe we'll have a big snow before Christmas." She chatted on amiably about the weather.

The room was "pack-jam" full. It contained two beds, one iron and one wooden. One was painted sky blue, the other walnut. In the room also was a walnut dresser with a cracked mirror, a scarred white washstand with a dull mirror, two brown trunks which were new in 1880, an old sewing machine with a broken pedal, a small wood range, a cracked wood heater, a wobbly-legged dining table with a frayed white oilcloth, two long unpainted benches, a small table, and about ten straight chairs. The floor was clean and bare. On a rough plank shelf in the corner stood an eight-day clock and near it sat a grinning cat family. On the small table was a cracked blue pitcher.

"The pitcher's really no good now," said Sarah, "but it's too pretty to throw away. It ain't been cracked but a week. Last summer we kept it full of fresh wildflowers. We kept them in quart fruit jars, too, but we called the blue pitcher our Sunday vase. It's very little of pretty things we ever have. We don't have time to work no flowers so we have to use the wild ones."

She fingered the white scrim curtains. "I do wish we could afford some real lace curtains but I've done give up hope of that. I used to hope that some day we could have things but times gits worser and worser. We ain't never had nothing and we won't never have nothing.

"All of our folks before us was tenant farmers and that's all we've ever done. If you know anything about tenant farming you know they do without everything all the year hoping to have something in the fall. Well, it's very little they ever have, but it's a hope to live and work for all the year just the same. I was raised hard and so was John. We had plenty to eat and that was all. No nice clothes and never a cent to throw away. The first years after John and me got married was hard a-plenty but they ain't nothing to what we've had lately.

"We started off on a ten-acre farm, four acres of tobacco, two of cotton and four acres of corn. That didn't include the garden and the 'tater patch. We raised enough vegetables, hogs, and chickens for us, and our money crop bought the rest — you know, sugar, coffee, and a piece of clothes now and then.

"We worked early and late that first year and we made a good crop. In a little over a year after we married Lucy come, and as she come in August I won't worth much to John the whole year. He was good to me, too, and tried to keep me out of the field when I was so heavy.

"The next year I worked like a nigger and that fall John bought me a coat suit, come the time he sold the first load of tobacco. If he'd waited till the last load I wouldn't of got one because the last load got wet and we got just $35 for it when it was worth pretty near $200. The coat suit didn't do me much good that winter because I was in the family way again and it was the next winter before I could wear it. John bought hisself a suit of clothes, too, and he shore was proud of it because it was the first whole suit he ever had.

"Macy was born in March and I was pretty sick. John was mighty disappointed because he had his heart sot on a boy. He said that the younguns was coming too fast and that with more mouths to feed and me not able to work half the time we'd soon find ourselves starving to death.

"It just about got John's goat and he commenced to drink harder. He'd always drunk some but now he was like a hog in a bucket of slops. He suddenly got the notion that he wanted to git rid of me and the younguns and he'd raise hell and try to fight when he got drunk. He was mighty kind to us when he was sober but he worried about how to take care of us. Then I got big again.

"I would rather of done near 'bout anything than to had to tell him about it. There was a old granny woman in our neighborhood — she's dead now — and she told me to drink cotton root tea. She swore that that would knock it up, and it did but I liked to of died. John finally made me tell the truth and he cried and said that it was his sin instead of mine. He is funny like that. He didn't think it was wrong to cuss, drink, and work me to death, but he thought it was awful to git rid of a baby or to impose on a dumb animal. He would lie to me, too, but he thought stealing was the worst of all the crimes. Well, I was mighty slow in gitting well but he was good to me and didn't rush me to the field.

"He didn't say a word when I told him a few months atter that we was going to have another one. He just kissed me kinda slow and he said, 'God knows, Sarah, I love the brats but I'm worried about how to look atter them.' I told him that they'd be a way and he brightened up a little.

"Well, sir, when Jack was born John was tickled pink. For several months he didn't drink a drop but when he sold the last load of tobacco he found out that they won't going to be a cent left atter the bills was paid so he spent it all on a drunk and let the bills go to the Old Harry.[1]

"He come home about midnight as drunk as a dog and as broke as a beggar." The big woman looked down at her knotted hands. "I suddenly took a notion that I could beat the stuffin' out of him, and I did. I got a barrel stave and I turned him across the table bench and I blistered his rump. I made him pretty sore but it ain't done no good yet 'cause he still gits drunk even in spite of the doctor tellin' him that it would kill him.

"When Jack was two years old the twins come. It had got harder to feed the new mouths and even if John had been mighty worried all the time I never did worry till Amy and Joyce got here; then I was in despair. We hadn't paid the doctor for bringing Jack yet and we still owed a little on Macy. He charged us double the usual price when he brought the twins and from that minute on ever' bill has doubled it seems like.

"Them was my last because before they was a year old I had appendicitis and when the doctor operated he tied my tubes so I couldn't have no more.

"John had his appendix cut out a few years atter that and all of them bills ain't been paid yet.

"It was lucky for us that our younguns was pretty healthy. They all had measles, whooping cough, chicken pox, and mumps and all the other diseases that younguns is supposed to have. The only things that won't perfectly natural happened to Amy. She was born with a crooked foot but she won't born with yellow fever. She had it though when she was five. We thought that we'd lose her then in spite of the devil but she got well. God bless the government — it had Amy's crooked leg operated on two years ago and it's as good as Joyce's now.

"The county woman found out about her leg from her schoolteacher and she come to me about it. Well sir, I said right off that the child was a-going to git that chance, but John was just as determined that she shouldn't. I finally won and we sent her off to Raleigh. It like to a-broke my heart that I couldn't at least go with her, but we didn't have no money. We didn't see her for ten weeks, but she could walk straight then. Since it healed we can't tell that it was ever crooked.

"All of us is in good health now and even if we don't have enough to eat all the time and nothing to wear but rags I am gladder of our health than money.

---

[1] The Devil.

"We wanted our children to git a education because me and Pa can't neither one read nor write, and we know how not having a education can keep you out of a job, from teaching in Sunday school, and from 'sociating with good people. Me and John both went to school for a few months, but that won't enough for us to learn nothing. We was too pore to help the younguns through high school. When Lucy got to the sixth grade we had to stop her because they was so much work to do, what with the farm work, the housework, the twins, and all. She stayed home four years and helped me, then she got a job in a store in Goldsboro and went to work. I reckon she had been clerking about a year when she married a civil engineer and moved off to Raleigh.

"Macy finished the sixth grade the year Anne went to work so she had to stay home and help me. She got married when she was seventeen; married a farmer who won't worth his salt. She left him a heap of times but now he's doing pretty good. They've got seven younguns. Jack quit school in the fifth grade to help his pa on the farm. He got married two years ago. Amy and Joyce is sixteen now and they can't go on in the ninth grade this year because we ain't got money to buy books and the stuff they need to learn to cook and sew. I wish we did have.

"We just played the devil by not farming this year. We thought that we'd make a whole heap more working out by the day but we found out different pretty quick. A heap of folks wanted work done but they ain't had no money on hand. A heap of them give us vegetables and stuff for our work. Some of them hired us on a-credit to chop cotton and barn and grade tobacco. When the boll weevil eat the cotton up they thought that we was no better to lose than them. When tobacco brought little prices they thought that we hadn't orter charge for our work.

"We are going to farm this land around here next year and so we don't have to pay no rent nor for wood we burn. It shore is a big help, too, not to have to pay for them things when gitting a little to eat's such a problem.

"We've got a 1924 Dodge sedan but it ain't much good no more, even if we had the money to run it. We made a good crop in 1924 and that fall John bought the car. He was drunk when he bought it and he bent a fender before he got it home. We ain't never had no radio. The house is wired for lights but we can't never afford it. We git water from the pump out there in the back yard. Our toilet is off there to the left and, if I do say so, it's kept clean. We take a daily wash in spots and every Saturday night we bring the big tin tub in and all takes a good hot bath. The girls bathe during the week sometimes when their pa goes off.

"Diet? Well now, I don't know. I always thought that just so a person eat a-plenty it didn't matter much what he eat. Of course I think vegetables, eggs, milk, and butter is good for folks and I believe in plenty of hot coffee in cold weather. Then I believe that corn bread is better for a body than biscuits. We always did have enough of something till the last year or so. My worry's not diet but where to git any kind of rations from.

"Well sir, it's been a good while since I thought of religion. I used to belong to the Baptist Church but I've always been used to cussing, drinking, and working on Sunday. I know a whole heap of times in the busy season when we done our week's washing, scrubbing, and cleaning on a-Sunday and thought nothing of it. I stopped going to church mostly way back when the younguns was little. You see, I didn't have nothing to wear for me nor them. It was a good ways to go and John wouldn't go with me nor keep the younguns for me to go. He never did care for churches nor religion and way atter awhile the hard life took everything outen me 'cept cussing, I reckon.

"I ain't never voted, but John's a Democrat. He ain't never let me vote but he thinks it's a woman's place to cut wood and stay all night in a mean neighborhood by herself. Two or three times I have had to defend our stuff with a shotgun when he was away, and he laughs and says that taking a man's place at home is all right but a man's place in voting is all wrong. There comes John now and I've got to cook dinner." She bounded out of her chair and began building a fire in the stove.

Just then John came puffing in with a small armful of wood. He is extremely stout and low and has a round jolly face. His hair is nearly snow white but he does not look his fifty-three years. He has jolly brown eyes, red cheeks, and wide mouth. Taken all in all, he reminds one of a fat and mischievous elf.

"Why howdy," he greeted his guest royally. "Just keep your cheer and make yourself to home. I thought I heard you hens talking politics as I come up." He continued briskly, "I'm a Democrat; I stand for the New Deal and Roosevelt. I am for the WPA, the NYA, the NRA, the AAA, the FHA, and crop control. I'm going to vote for control in December. We've got mighty little of the government money but I'm still saying that the WPA, CCC,[2] and all the rest is shore doing a big part for North Carolina. The government shore give us enough when it paid for Amy's leg operation.

"I'm supposed to be one of the best farmers in Wilson County and I know that I'm going to make a good crop next year. Did you know

[2] The Civilian Conservation Corps, a quasi-military corps developed in the early New Deal that placed unemployed young people in camps to work on conservation projects around the country.

that the best tobacco plants air raised on new ground land? They air, and the land's got to be burnt over for the best results. I usually fix it in the wintertime, that is, I clear the land up and burn the brush in December or January. I plow the land deep with a two-horse plow along about the first of February, rake out the roots and grass and plant the seed thick. I roll logs up to each side of the bed and pull the canvas tight across it.

"It don't need no more attention then till long about the middle of March or the first of April when the plants has to be thinned out and the weeds pulled out. Long about that time I break up my tobacco patch with a two-horse plow, harrow it good, and run the rows. I want at least a half a ton of good guano³ to the acre and when I git it out I feel like I'm really starting to farm. 'Bout the first of May, if it's warm, or later if it ain't, I set out my plants. That's when my whole family commences to git busy shore 'nuff.

"We use good strong lightard⁴ pegs to stick the holes and one sets out about as fast as a feller can drop the plants. I want them about two and a half feet apart and I want the dirt packed tight to the roots. If it's real dry we water them with buckets and gourds.

"In about four weeks we go over and loosen the dirt around the roots with a hoe and then we plow it. We have to do this two or three times before time to lay by.

"'Bout the time we git through chopping and plowing the first time, the worms commences to chaw on it and the little suckers start to grow. Them suckers and worms can ruin a tobacco patch pronto so we all gits busy killing them worms and pulling out them suckers. Man, that's some job! Atter we've gone over it two or three times it starts flowering out and then we've got to top it, too.

"Well, 'long in early July the lugs gits to turning yaller and we go out there and crap off the ripe leaves. The slides hauls it to the barn and the women and children and a few men hands it, strings it, and puts it in the barn. When all the racks are full or when we git all the tobacco crapped we quit for the day. Then we fire up and for several days we cure it. When the stems are dry so they are brown and crack easy when broke, we take it out of the barn and pack it up in the packhouse or the house we live in. We go over and worm, sucker, and top once more; then we barn the body

---

³ Bat or bird excrement, imported from South America and widely used as a fertilizer.

⁴ Lightard (lighterd), or lightwood, is a southern term for dead, seasoned pine, especially from roots or fallen limbs. Thanks to its high resin content, it burns with a brilliant light, hence the name; the resin also makes it quite hard, rendering the pegs useful for drilling holes in the soil to transplant tobacco seedlings.

leaves. Then we sucker, worm, and top once more before barning the tips.[5]

"When the curing is done we start to grading. The younguns takes it off the sticks while two people puts it in three or four grades. As many as wants to can tie it in bundles with another leaf of tobacco, and then the younguns puts it up on dressed sticks. The lugs, body, and tips cured in each barn are kept in separate piles and sold that way. As fast as we git a barn graded I carry it off and sell it.

"Raising cotton is more trouble than tobacco, but I always raise some. I break up the land in March and put out the fertilizer. I plant the seeds during April usually, but we used to plant it in March. May's not too late, though.

"The first chopping is the biggest trouble because the plants has got to be chopped to the right stand. I like for them to be a foot apart. As soon as it's chopped it has got to be plowed. We do this about three times before July or August when we lay it by.

"We leave it alone until the bolls starts to opening in September, then we go out with clean guano sacks and pick that cotton. Did you ever pick cotton? Well, let me tell you, the burs sticks your fingers, scratches your hands and legs all over, and it ain't impossible to git stung by a stinging worm. When it turns cold, which it's apt to do before the last picking, your hands pretty near freeze off.

"As we pick it we put it in the packhouse and as fast as we pick a bale I carry it to the gin.[6] Soon's it's ginned I haul it to the market and sell it. They ain't no money much in cotton no more.

"Corn's easy to raise. All you have to do is plant it in April and plow it a couple of times. 'Long about November, maybe in October, you have to gather it. Sometimes, when I have time, I pull my fodder[7] or top it 'long

---

[5] This paragraph uses a number of technical terms to describe tobacco farming. Lugs are the lowest leaves on a tobacco stalk, the lowest-grade leaves of the plant, and the first to ripen (turn yellow). Crap is a variant form of crop, here a verb meaning "to harvest." To worm, sucker, and top were the farmer's chief tasks in the latter part of the cultivation season for tobacco — to keep the plants pruned by removing the blossoms at the top of the plant and the secondary growths, or "suckers" (which diverted growth from the more valuable leaves), and to remove the tobacco hornworms that appeared about the same time. To barn is to place the harvested leaves, strung on sticks, in the tobacco barn for curing. In this part of North Carolina, tobacco was *flue-cured,* i.e., cured by intense heat generated by a furnace attached to the barn and transmitted to the air of the interior by flues.

[6] The cotton gin (short for engine) was a machine that separated cotton fibers from cotton seed. The first gin successfully performing this process on upland, or short-staple cotton (the chief form in which it was grown in the South) was invented in 1793 by Eli Whitney and helped make possible the creation and expansion of the vast southern Cotton Belt in the nineteenth century.

[7] To pull fodder means to strip corn stalks of their leaves for use as animal food.

about July. I need the fodder all the time but it comes off in tobacco barning time and we're pretty busy.

"Sarah will have a half a acre of sweet potatoes, a half acre of Irish potatoes, and a big garden always. Sometimes I fuss about it, but law, the vegetables comes in handy. She says that I'm a bad drunkard but she don't know nothing. She ought to have some men I know. I did git drunk the last load of tobacco year before last, and I spent $13 somehow. Shucks though, that ain't nothing; a heap of men spends the last cent they gits.

"I'll say it for Sarah, though; she has been a good wife through thick and thin and I don't know of none that's better." He looked at her affectionately. "She does raise a heap of hell sometimes, though."

He folded his stubby hands across his paunchy stomach and quietly said, "We don't always have enough to eat but me and Sarah both knows that times will git better. We've had depressions before and we've had to play the game a few times lately.

"What game? Well it's a heap of fun even if the belly is holler. You see, when rations gits slim we just have two meals a day or maybe we'll just have a cup of coffee for breakfast. While we drink the coffee we poke the fun at rich people and pretend that we are having just what we want. We ask each other polite-like to have toast and jelly and bacon and eggs and it shore helps.

"When we have cereal for breakfast or meat and bread we don't have no dinner at all and we have supper at four o'clock. As we set down to the table we play like all of us had been to dinner with friends. We ask each other what he had and we all make out we had turkey, chicken, cake, pie, and a heap of other fancy stuff. Sometimes when one's telling what he had somebody will say, 'That's funny, I had the same thing.' You'd be surprised how much that helps out.

"Lucy married right well off, but she ain't got nothing to help us with because her husband's people lives with them and they try to put some in the bank. We had to help Macy till we got so we couldn't; now she manages without us. Jack is gitting a slow start, but he can't help us none. The twins ain't got no jobs. They ain't got much clothes either, so when one goes a- visiting she takes pretty near all the clothes and the one that's left ain't got a half decent rag.

"I'm sorry my younguns can't git a education because that is the one thing a feller has got to have to git a job. Shucks, you can't dig ditches now unless you got a high school education and you can't put up a hawg pasture unless you got a college education. I wish things was back where they useter be when a feller just had to be strong and honest and have a little horse sense to git any kind of job.

"Sales tax is the biggest shame in North Carolina, especially when money gits missing from the Revenue Department and nobody can find out who took it. Well, I don't care much for the gas chamber at Raleigh either, but we have to have something I reckon.

"I'm proud of North Carolina, too, and I don't like for our President to call it no problem 'cause it ain't as much a problem as some of the other states what air running over with foreigner gangsters. The biggest problem I see here is the landlord that has a bunch of tenant farmers on his place. They work like niggers all the year and he gits rich. They can't even make enough to eat on through the winter. I've had some pretty good landlords and some pretty bad ones but I reckon that I'll have to put up with them all my life. I hate the thieving rogues anyhow, good or bad. I'm proud of our United States though, and every time I hear the 'Star-Spangled Banner' I feel a lump in my throat. There ain't no other nation in the world that would have sense enough to think of WPA and all the other A's.

"Oh, you want to talk religion too, huh? Well, I ain't much on that. I ain't never joined no church and I ain't been much either, but I told my family to go ahead. I'd be glad if they went to church. I ain't tried to teach them no Bible 'cause if I can't read, how am I gonna know that what I hear is in the Bible?"

Sarah, who was calmly putting corn bread in a large iron griddle, broke in. "You set a pore example, John, and you know it. I did, too, for that matter, a-cussin' and swearin' and saying things I hadn't ought to. I always told the younguns, though, not to cast stones at people lest somebody throw bricks at them. I wanted them to be educated, kind, polite, and humblesome. I'm not disappointed; I'm just sorry we couldn't give them a better start."

"I maybe did set a pore example," John resumed, "but I shore didn't tell them to foller in my footsteps. Besides, I ain't altogether spared the rod. I'm right proud of them in a way. Of course, we ain't got but one boy but he don't drink and he ain't never been in jail.

"Speaking about money; well, I reckon we live on about four or five dollars a week now but it ain't exactly what you call living. I git a day's work here and yonder digging ditches or wells, chopping wood, or killing hogs. Some of them pay me off in meat or potatoes. Some weeks we don't have but a dollar or two and so we go in debt for groceries and have to pay it out of the next week's money. We've never had more than about twelve dollars a week to live on except in wartime and you know the high prices of everything then. I think we could do good on fifteen dollars a week and pay our bills good, don't you, Sarah?"

"I'd say so," Sarah nodded smiling. "We could live fine on that. Why we might even be able atter a while to buy some lace curtains."

John rebuked her gently. "It's no time to be thinking of lace curtains, honey, and us without half enough to eat."

"Oh," she said slowly, "oh, I'd forgot just about a minute where I was."

John coughed gruffly. "You're gonna have lace curtains someday, Sarah. Just as shore as God spares my life for a little while longer you're gonna have them lace curtains."

WALTER ROWLAND

"Ain't Got No Screens": A Black Tenant Family, Arkansas

Sho' ain' goin' to stay hyar no longer, ain't got no screens.

They were seated on the front porch of a three-room, unpainted shack. She, a portly Negress, was comfortably anchored in a swing behind a veil of honeysuckle vines. He was draped languidly about a tilted, cane-bottom chair, one leg of which was perilously near a gaping hole in the floor.

"Come in, suh," he unwrapped himself from his chair, and hastily brought another, which he placed safely away from the hole. "Dat noon breeze comes thoo hyar. Hit's fine, too, dese hot days.

"No, suh, I ain' been to de fiel' dis mornin', jus' puckerin' aroun' de house a bit; hit's mos' too wet to work in de fiel' — little mo' rain and dey won't be no cotton, though dey ain' been near de rain we had de year of de Big Flood[8] —

"What year was de Big Flood, honey? It was de yeah after we come up fum Mississippi — must've been twenty-seb'm. And rain! Dey wuz fifteen families on ouah place; de landlord got his stuff out to high land, and he never left nothin' to hep us git out cepn' two ole pieces of waggins and a no 'count team of mules dat wouldn' pull more'n fo' men.

"Ain't Got No Screens," in Tom E. Terrill and Jerrold Hirsch, eds., *Such as Us: Southern Voices of the Thirties* (Chapel Hill: University of North Carolina Press, 1978), 54 – 57.
    [8] The 1927 flood of the Mississippi River covered 20,000 square miles, drove 300,000 people from their homes, and left 246 dead [note from Terrill and Hirsch, *Such as Us*].

"Time hit come my turn, water wuz up to de wagin bed, and I couldn' see de road, though I knowed whar it was; but you know, long's I been on de farm I cain't drive a team 'til yet, and I got 'em too fur to one side 'tween two dreens, en de wagin tumpled over in de deep water, en we lost practick'ly all we 'cumulated, furniture en all.

"I give up de bottoms den; hit's better land, but I got be where I kin git out when I wants to git out.

"You say dis land look like bottomland to you? Co'se hit's black and strong and level, but hit's a heap higher dan de bottoms, I tell you!

"How do we farm? Well, dey's sev'ul diff'unt ways. Dare is de cash rentuh, but we has always sharecropped, on a third and a four — he furnish de house en de land en credicks you enough to live on, en den you settles at de end of de year. In de cotton we gives him a fourth, in de cawn he gits a third — ain' dat right, honey?" he asked his wife. "Anyhow, when you raise four bales of cotton de landlord gits one en you git three, and if you raise three wagonloads of cawn he gits de first one en you git the other two.

"Landlord's got a store on de place, en he 'low you so much a week on de books — dey wuz four in my family and he didn' 'low us but a twenty-four-poun' sack of flouah, en a twenty-four-poun' sack of meal, en eight poun's of lard, en maybe a bar of soap. Ef you got molasses you didn' git no sugah, en ef you got bakin' powdah you didn' git no sody — Meat? Whooo! We didn' git no meat, but we'd ketch a mess of fish now en den, en de nex' year we had ouah own meat.

"De landlord wouldn' give us no land foh a garden, er no wire to fence it, ef we could of got some land. He ain' like Mistuh Brewer down de road. Mistuh Brewer give his 'croppers land foh a garden, en if dey use it he doan' charge 'em no rent, but ef dey doan' use it he makes 'em pay rent on it, eight dollars an acre — but we had to plant cotton right up to de do'.

"Tolbert — dat's my oldes' — hired out sometimes drivin' tractor — he got six bits a day foh workin' fum kin to cain't, fum sunup to sundown. He got a dollah a day foh a while, but den dey put him back on six bits. No, suh, when it rain en he cain' work he doan' git no six bits for *dat* day. Tolbert he kin do anything to a tractor, he kin take one down and put it back up, en he kin tell jus' by listenin' what's wrong with one; learned it all jus' by studyin' a 'struction book. No, suh, you see, dey doan' use no colored mechanics hyar in Holly Grove, en I guess he woan' never git nothin' but six bits a day. Yas, suh, I guess he *could* go off somewhare, but I doan' speck he will —

"We misses screens de mos' aroun' dis place, pesky flies and mosquitoes is so bad. I said sump'n about it to Mr. Sparrow early dis spring, but

I guess he forgot — or mebbe he ain' forgot, he jus' doan' *want* us to have no screens. Jus' like I wanted a patch of sorghum, make me some 'lasses with, but he say hit sour the land. What he mean was, hit sour dat ninety cents a bucket he gits for Steamboat.[9]

"Most of us is credick men — you gives a dime foh a nickel box of matches, and a dime foh a nickel bah of soap — mebbe two foh fifteen, en you kin git flouah en meal in town foh about half whut it cost you out'n the comm'sary. We-el, yas, suh, I meant de cash price in town, dey ain' no credick in town, less'n yo' landlord stand good, en den dey marks you up en he git a percent off'n you. Sometimes where dey ain' no sto' on the plantation all de landlords goes in and buys stock in de sto' in town, en hit's jus' de same.

"De landlord is landlord, de politicians is landlord, de judge is landlord, de shurf is landlord, ever'body is landlord, en we ain' got nothin'!

"You take de acre p'duction checks de gov'munt gives foh not plantin' cotton:[10] fust dey wuz made out so's we couldn' git 'em thout de landlord — dey wuz even sent to him — en he mark 'em up en mark 'em down, en mark you up in de comm'sary en mark you down, en den we didn't git no checks, we jus' signed en git whut he *say* we had comin'. En de landlord think he ought to have *all* the acre p'duction checks, cause it his land, en we oughtn' to git nothin', but de Tenant Farmers' Union[11] put up a kick, en now dey send *us* de checks — ef we evah git anoth'un. *Who* gives de checks out? I doan' know *who*, jus' de gov'munt. But dey comes thoo de county board, en dey is all landlords —

"I thinks mebbe nex' year I'll git a place on Sebastian McElroy's farm — he's a colored man — en he's mo' apt to treat me right, en den I kin have a garden, en a patch o' peanuts, en some Arsh 'taters, en some sweet 'taters; en Sebastian got screens on all his houses. I'd lots ruther work for a colored landlord than a white man one.

"I had a old Hudson Super Six two years ago, but hit tuck so much gas, en I spent all mah cash money en they come and tuck hit back foh de payments. I mos' gin'ally clears about seventy-five dollahs. Sometimes I

[9] A brand of molasses.

[10] Attempting to raise farm incomes by preventing overproduction of crops such as cotton, New Deal farm programs originated the practice of paying farmers to take acreage out of staple-crop cultivation. In the Cotton South, however, where most of those working the land were landless tenants or sharecroppers, a persistent controversy concerned the definition of "farmer"; did it include tenants and sharecroppers, or were these simply employees of their landlords, and thus ineligible to receive production checks? As the interviewee notes, eligibility was determined by local boards dominated by local landlords, who usually resolved the issue at the expense of their tenants and croppers.

[11] The Southern Tenant Farmers' Union, a vigorous but short-lived tenant farmer organization that was strongest in Oklahoma and Arkansas. [Note from Terrill and Hirsch, *Such as Us.*]

doan', though; sometimes I comes out in de hole. But I'm goin' to move nex' year again; ef I doan' git on Sebastian's place, I'm goin' to git on somebody else's. Sho' ain' goin' to stay hyar no longer, ain't got no screens."

IDA MOORE

"Old Man Dobbin and His Crowd": White Cotton-Mill Workers, North Carolina

It was payday at the mill and Old Man Dobbin had drawn his last check. He held the little blue slip in his hand and not paying any attention to me or to his wife or to his two grandchildren he read the figures again and spoke aloud. "Five dollars and ninety-three cent and a dollar and sixty-three cent of it took out for rent. Never got in but two days last week. It ain't so much, but it's goin' to push us to get along any sort of way without it."

"It'll shore be hard, but then its near 'bout always been hard," his wife said in a slow, twanging voice.

Her statement was one beyond which none of us could for the moment pass. We sat there in a semicircle around the little laundry stove which furnished heat for the small room, and my mind reviewed the conversation I had had not more than fifteen minutes before with the man who was passing the Dobbin home. "That house there? That's where old man Dobbin and his crowd lives," he'd said. "They's twelve or thirteen of 'em, I forget which, livin' there now. More'n likely you'll find the old man hisself at home. I heard tell they laid him off the other day. George Dobbin's his name. Yessum, he's got children aworkin', but I wouldn't be surprised if the old man don't need his job too to get along on."

George Dobbin shifted his chair a little further from the stove. "Yessir, it's goin' to be hard to get along and me not aworkin'," he said.

"How did you lose your job?" I asked.

"Well, as you can see, I'm agettin' old. Be sixty-eight comin' June. But

"Old Man Dobbin and His Crowd," in Federal Writers' Project, *These Are Our Lives* (Chapel Hill: University of North Carolina Press, 1939), 187 – 213.

I coulder held out if my age hader been all was against me. Seven year ago a automobile struck me when I was crossin' the street down yonder in front of the comp'ny store and I was right bad injured. It laid me up for three months and left me with a game leg once I did get about again. They give me a elevator job when I went back to the mill but awhile back when they took a spell of stretchin' the stretchout they cut out my job and divided the elevator runnin' amongst the four ropin' haulers. And they put me on a job of sweepin' and haulin' and cleanin' that would just about finish up airy forty-five year old man I know. I stuck to it for a day and when I come home that night my whole entire body hurt me so I couldn't lay in bed atall. The next mornin' I went to my bossman and asked him if they wasn't some lighter job he could put me on for maybe lower pay. And he answered me, 'You've got as light a job as they are in the mill. The New Deal's made all mill jobs heavy.' He never explained what he meant and I've been awonderin' since what he had in his mind. Then he told me if I wanted a job I'd have to keep the one I was on, and I says to him, 'If I tried to keep it up it'd most likely kill me and if by a miracle it happened not to kill me it'd lay me up in bed for six months with big doctor bills for my children to pay. Since I see trouble abrewin' if I stay on,' I says to him, 'I'll nip it in the bud before it matures by quittin' right now.' When you get disabled to do hard work, they want to get rid of you and they know how. And so, I reckin this here is the last mill check I'll ever draw."

George Dobbin slipped the piece of paper into the pocket of his old brown coat. He removed his battered brown hat and sat hunched over with his big-knuckled hands pushing fingertip to fingertip and then quickly pulling them apart. Obviously he had never been a very large man, but as I looked at him I had the feeling that for a number of years he must have been dwindling away with pernicious regularity to have reached his present emaciated state. His energetic voice and his equally live gestures did not seem to belong to the puny-looking body from which they came.

"Have you lived here many years?" I asked George.

"I moved to Rimmerton eighteen year ago and every one of my crowd learnt up in the mill down yonder. Up till then it'd been me and the old lady to make a livin' for all and we had plenty strugglin' adoin' it.

"We started off farmin' and stuck to it up to the fall of 1913 and '14. That year we planted cotton on a fourteen cent basis and got six cent for some and four and a half for the rest. Europe had got started in the war and the countries that had put in orders for cotton countermanded 'em and flooded our home market. Me and Sally made fourteen bales of cotton, thirty-one barrels of corn, and three hundred bushels of potatoes besides a sight of peas. It was one of the best crop years I ever knowed in Johnson County and we come out about the porest we ever done. We worked let me tell you, we worked to make that crop."

"Law, I reckin we did. I hoed seventeen acres of cotton by myself without one lick of help except for the little grass pickin' done by the geese, done my housework, and looked after three children. Many a night after supper I'd scour my floors or do my washin' and have it ready so's I could put it on the line before I went to the field at sun-up next mornin'. In gatherin' time I'd take my little baby to the field and put him in a wooden box at the end of a cotton row of a early mornin' when the frost lay thick as snow on the ground. Me and George picked every boll that went into eight bales of that cotton and I never got so much as two yards of ten-cent apron gingham."

"We didn't pick the last bale," George said, "and I never seen prettier cotton in a field. I'd hauled thirteen bales to the gin and hadn't brought back a cent. Mr. Wilson, my landlord, got half of it because the land was his'n and he took the other half to pay for what rashins he'd furnished. Me and the old woman was busy tryin' to get the peas picked and the potatoes dug so's to have somethin' to live on and I had no notion of stoppin' to pick that last bale of cotton. I said to Mr. Wilson, 'Now, they's some pretty cotton down there in the field, and it's all yourn and on yore land. I've wore out and I've not got time to pick it neither and pickin's sixty cent a hundred. They's not enough money at my house to pay for the pickin' of one hundred pound. If you want your cotton you better see to gettin' it out.' Mr. Wilson said, 'I'll get some hands in there and get that cotton ready for ginnin', but if I don't come out on it, I'll charge up half the loss against you.' And I answered him like this, 'Mr. Wilson, you charge it if you want to but it'll be what's called a dead debt. I ain't gonna work like a mule raisin' fourteen bales of cotton off of which I've got nare cent and then pay somebody extry money because I was fool enough to raise it.'

"He come back to me a few days later and he said, 'We come out four dollars in the hole on that bale and yore part is two dollars. I thought maybe you'd just let the shoulder of meat I borrowed from you when you killed that hog the other day go to settle up with me.'

"I felt right sorry I was a human then. I looked at him and I said, 'Mr. Wilson, I loaned you that meat thinkin' of course you'd pay it back. But if you want it that bad keep it.' He kept it.

"And it's hard to believe, but a few days later he come to my house and said half of my four hogs was his because I'd fed 'em out of the crop."

"Yessir, he done that thing, he did for sure, and me and George had cut weeds to feed them hogs and we give 'em corn we'd made the year before. He'd got everything we'd growed on the land but a few potatoes and peas and then wanted half the hogs."

"I'd rented corn land," George said, "on the terms of one dollar for every barrel I made and me furnishin' the fertilizer. We come out even on the corn.

"I said to Wilson when he asked me for the hogs, 'Do your mortgage call for hogs' — he'd took a mortgage against my half of the crop before he'd furnish me you know. 'No, the mortgage don't call for 'em but if you think about it honest you know they're mine.' I answered him with, 'Take everything your paper calls for but I'd advise you to leave the rest alone.' He never got my hogs.

"We had them peas and potatoes and hogs and no clothes atall to face the rest of the winter with. Good luck come to me though, and in February I left the farm and went to public work. The Nursery Company at Turnersville give me the job of stable-boss and paid me $30 a month and furnished a house to live in too. That wage did seem powerful good after the long hard year of work that hadn't cleared us a nickel. I reckin it must've been about July when I got a chance at a better job."

"It was August, George. I remember it was three weeks after the twins was born we moved to Henderson."

"Mills was beginnin' to pay good," George continued. "It wa'n't long till I was makin' $20 a week."

"We done some good livin' then," Sally remarked. "It seemed like we never had to study and contrive so hard. I could buy all the milk my children needed."

"Groceries kept agoin' up," George began again, "and they took up most of the wages, but then we did have enough to eat.

"In 1919 we moved to Durham and first thing I knowed I was makin' from 25 to 35 dollars a week. Times stayed good with us up to '21. When I say times was good I don't mean we done no fancy livin' atall but we set down to the table three times a day and always found somethin' on it.

"Then one day I went in the mill and seen a notice tellin' of a twenty-five percent cut and a shortenin' of time to three days a week. Hard times really set in like always groceries never come down accordin' to the cut."

"Them was miserable days for us," Sally declared, "and many a time my little ones cried for milk."

"And when it begin to look like the livin' wa'n't worth the worry of gettin' along I lost my job complete — left without ary little piece of a job.

"It was human kindness that caused me to lose it too. A body is hard put to it to understand how kindness can work against him sometimes but it sure happens. Word got out amongst the neighbors that we was havin' a struggle gettin' along with me one workin' and seven children lookin' to me for a livin'. First thing we knowed a woman come out and set to talk awhile with my wife. She asked her how we managed to live on what I made and the old lady answered we done the best we could. At different times three women come out and done just about such talk as the first one and Sally, she answered 'em all alike, but not ary time did she ever ask help of 'em. But it wasn't long till baskets of groceries started comin' to us and it seemed just like manna from heaven. That'd been goin' on a few weeks when my boss told me Mr. Wilder, the superintendent, wanted to see me.

"Soon as I could I went to Mr. Wilder's office and told him Mr. Henry said he wanted to see me. He answered right quick, 'Yes, Dobbin, I did. The comp'ny's decided all who can't live sumptuous on what they make at this mill is to be given ten-day notice. I'm givin' you yores now.'

"'But Mr. Wilder,' I says, 'I don't understand what's causin' this. I have never raised one word of complaint against this mill.'

"'Mr. Dobbin, it's awful knockin' on the mill,' he says, 'to have folks workin' for this company that calls on the welfare and the Salvation Army for help. We don't like to have the Salvation Army callin' up this office and tellin' us they'd like a contribution from us to help them take care of our hands.'

"I looked at Mr. Wilder settin' there behind his desk and I knowed he couldn't help feelin' I was tellin' the truth when I spoke. 'Before God, Mr. Wilder,' I said, 'to my ricollection I've never spoke to a Salvation Army man or woman in my life and I've never been to no organization to ask for help.'

"'But you've been agettin' help, ain't you?" he asked.

"'I've got help and I highly appreciate it,' I said. 'It's kept my children from goin' hungry.'

"'You've got your notice,' he answered me.

"I took some of the money I drawed that week and bought me a ticket to New Falls. Had a brother livin' here then and he took me to his bossman and helped me get the promise of a house and job. But I knowed it cost money to move and I thought to myself it won't hurt none to go to Mr. Richards, the general manager, and see if he won't be more reasonable in his ways than Mr. Wilder.

"On a Wednesday I went. And I says to him, 'Mr. Richards, I want to ask you, do you find fault with my work and my way and manner of livin'?'

"'None whatever, Mr. Dobbin,' he answered me.

"'Then why is my job bein' took away from me?' I asked him.

"'We may be doin' you a favor, Mr. Dobbin,' he said. 'It'll be for your own good if you can go somewhere else and get more time and better pay. The picture for this mill looks mighty gloomy. Have you got any notion where you're goin'?'

"'I've got a house and a job waitin' for me,' I said, 'but I've not got a copper to pay for movin'.'

"'Go out and hire you a truck,' he says, 'and charge it to the mill.'

"Well I couldn't get nothin' but a delivery truck and it wouldn't bring all of our furniture. When I went back to Mr. Richards he told me to have the balance crated, take it to the depot, and he'd pay the freight.

"You know them neighbors of mine crated everything I had and wouldn't let me raise my hand to help. They's never been no better people than them at that Durham mill."

"They's another thing they done always comes to my mind when I think of Durham," Sally said reflectively and her eyes looked beyond the two of us who listened.

"Two year before we left, when George was out one time with a sore foot, they'd come by our house after quittin' time of a evenin', them that worked in his departmint, and they'd drop coins in his hands till he had more'n he woulder made workin' that day. It's always stayed in my ricollection as a powerful sweet thing to've done." Her chair was rocking steadily now that she had ceased talking and her eyes were still gazing toward the hall.

"The welfare bought us train tickets and the neighbors fixed up dinner for us to eat on the train," George reminisced.

"They was cake and salmin balls and ham biscuits," Sally said. "Yes, they was a custard too."

"A old bachelor that boarded and never had no way of fixin' things bought the children some peppermint candy," George said. "I remember how the old lady worried with them twins tryin' to keep 'em from messin' up their clothes with the red off of that candy. That little Mary smeared it all over her face and Sally was washin' her when the train pulled into New Falls."

"We've been here at the Rimmerton Mill since," Sally said. "Twan't but a few months till Dan, our oldest, was fourteen and went in the mill with his pa. Now there's one good religious boy; anybody around'll tell you that. He never misses a Sunday goin' to church mornin' and night and of a evenin' too if they's preachin' goin' on. Pays no attention atall to the girls and uses his money to help out at home. He never got no education much on account of havin' to stay at home and help me with the other children, but he sure puts a heap of study on his Bible."

The last lingering tone of her monotonous voice trailed away into a silence, broken only by occasional sounds created by two small children who played in the rear of the room. Presently I became conscious of the movement of persons in the room overhead, listened as the sound became that of slow-moving feet descending stairs, and caught the jumbled noise of two girls talking as they moved through the hall outside. One suddenly ran ahead of the other and opened the front door. Her voice was loud as she said, 'Come on in Mrs. McBane.' A moment later three persons came into the room where Sally and George and I sat.

"Them's my two girls that stays at home," Sally said, "and that there is my friend neighbor, Mrs. McBane." Mrs. McBane, a massive woman wearing a sky blue coat, shoved herself across the room and sat down with measured gradualness in a chair near the ramshackle dresser. As the concluding move toward settling herself she brushed her bobbed hair away from her ruddy face and laid her hands comfortably at rest in her bulging lap.

"Hannah nor Venie neither can't seem to get on at the mill," Sally said referring to her two daughters who sat on the bed. "'Course, Hannah there has always had a bad head trouble and I don't know as she'd ever be able to work if she could get work to do. Her ears just takes spells of bleedin', and little pieces of what looks like bones comes out too."

Sally's words produced in Hannah such an acute embarrassment that she could not for the moment speak though her lips moved. Finally when she did speak it was in a cracked, nervous voice which except for the restraint forced upon it would have cried out rather than spoken out its words. "Mama, I wish you wouldn't be talkin' about my head," she declared. "Just cause my ears used to bleed you tell it like I still have head trouble. I can hear good as anybody now."

"Well, honey, you can't help it about your head and it ain't nothin' to be ashamed of," Sally said. "The doctors says your head ain't just like anybody else's but you shore ain't to blame for that. Her head treatmints and tonsils cost us $91 three year ago. She's not had the doctor in a right smart while now."

Hannah, unable to think of any further defense of her health, made a few final gestures of retreat. She brushed nervously at her frizzled yellow hair, shrugged her shoulders and stared out of the window.

"Hannah quit school when she was fourteen year old because it made her awful nervous," Sally was saying presently.

"I quit when I was fourteen too," Venie said, "but it was because I wanted a job. I've been waitin' five years for it and I guess I'll set here waitin' five more."

The suggestion of prolonged waiting instantly drew George out of his silence. "We'll all about perish before five year unless work picks up," he said. Venie giggled, but George, unmindful of interruption continued, "After I found out the mill was through with me I went up to the welfare and put in for a old age pension. The lady at the desk told me she'd have to wait to see what the legislature done about the appropriations for pensions before she could give me a answer. And when I asked her how long that'd be she said the first of July and I says to her, 'I'll be perished by then.' She laughed at that but t'wan't meant for no joke. Times is gettin hard for us."

"Taint like if they could make the full time the mill runs," Sally explained. "Now Dan, he'd make $10.08 if he worked four days but every week he's sent out to rest a day. Same with Mary and Louise. Mary's married now but her husband works in the chair factory at Jones Forks and she boards here like the rest that's workin'. She draws on the average of $9 a week and Louise draws about $7. Ruth, the mother of these two children you see here and one more that ain't come home from school, she makes the same as Mary. The four workin' pays me $5 a week apiece and I feed thirteen out of it and keep up best as I can with the rest of the debts housekeepin' makes. George's always went for wood and coal and rent and some for clothes. Now this week I can't get much board out of Mary and Louise because they both near 'bout had flu last week and never put in but a day apiece. They say it's all they can do to keep up with their work when they're well and to go down there sick would sure enough finish 'em up."

"I bet Ruth never missed nare day they'd let her work," Mrs. McBane said.

"No sirree," Sally answered. "I believe she'd go till she dropped in her tracks. She's at work today and her with a cold that ain't fur from pneumony but I couldn't keep her at home. She says a woman with three children to raise ain't got time to be sick. It's the same answer she makes when I try to get her to go to the sanitorium and be pleuriscoped. Beins her husband died with the tbs the doctor said her and the children both oughter be pleuriscoped ever six months, but she won't go. She says if she's got it she don't want to know it because with no money to take care of herself she'd die any way and knowin' it would make her worry and bring death on that much quicker. But she do cough awful of a night.

"Bud, he had the gallopin' kind, you know. Seemed like the more we done for him the faster it worked. Old Mrs. Smith over on 12th St. fixed him up a remedy that's guaranteed to cuore it but we couldn't see as it done Bud one bit of good. Some says they's nothin' you can do for the gallopin' kind nohow and I reckin they're right.

"These babies here, though, I do all I can to give 'em milk so's to build 'em up enough to keep 'em from havin' it. I worry more about Ruth than I do the children naturally since the work she has to do ain't none too good for her health nohow. Ruth never was no strong person but I always said she had more grit than anybody I knowed. I believe that's the children comin' now, ain't it George? It's past three o'clock."

"That there little Sarah'll let you know in a minute," George said, grinning. "First sound she ketches of Ruth atalkin' she'll make a beeline for the front door." And no sooner had he spoken than Sarah, the older of the two grandchildren, who had been trading doll chairs with her baby-sister, poised her head for listening, and the next moment scrambled to her feet and rushed out of the room.

"Of a pay day Ruth always brings her somethin'," Sally explained.

There was laughter in the hall and a child's grunt of pleasure, and the next instant, Sarah, leading the crowd, pranced into the room licking an ice-cream cone with great delight. The baby emitted a little squeal and stepped her feet high over the obstructing doll chair to reach her mother. Ruth bent down to pat the child on the head and to put into her outstretched hands the other cone she'd brought.

"This here is Ruth and that one's Mary and the other Louise though I doubt if you'll remember long which twin is which. George says they's times when he can't. That there is Dan." When Sally had finished introducing her daughters they looked about the room and fitted themselves in wherever they could. The twins, hardly more than five feet two and weighing not over ninety pounds, sat side by side on the further end of the bed. They had pert-looking narrow faces with pug noses, smooth skin, and eyes which must have been bright when less fatigued. Ruth, smaller than the twins, seeming so weary that she did not want to talk, slid into a chair in the corner partly shielded from view by Mrs. McBane. Dan went into the kitchen, came back occasionally to stand in the doorway listening to the conversation but never contributing to it.

And before the crowd had fully adjusted itself a small boy bearing two books and a tablet under his arm dashed into the room. Still panting, he stopped before Ruth and asked in great eagerness, "What'd you bring me, Mama?"

"I wasn't lookin' for you so soon," Ruth said. The Dobbins laughed and with greater abandon laughed Mrs. McBane.

The laughter was like a stinging blow to the child. Instantly he was sobbing and in his embarrassment he flung out his fists, pounding his mother and demanding a nickel. Before Ruth could calm him sufficiently to reach into her pocket, Mary came forth with a nickel and said, "Now be a little man, Johnny, and hush your cryin'. Your mama's got to save her money to pay her insurance with." The child took the nickel and his sniffles gradually died away to leave only the sound of an occasional shuffle of feet within the room.

"Talk like you ain't got no insurance to pay," Louise said to Mary.

"Well I never made enough this time to pay mine nohow," Mary answered.

"They's not a one of 'em," George began with a sweep of his arm which included Dan in the kitchen, "that draws much more'n half what they oughter." He batted his eyes and straightened himself in his chair. He looked about the room with a I-will-speak expression and began again to speak. "What labor's got to do is organize. I'd rather see it get its rights through laws but the laws they've got now is easy to get around. Seems like the union's the only chance."

"We joined the union durin' the strike," both twins spoke simultaneously. "All of us did."

George prepared himself for further speech. The presence of his children seemed to bolster his spirits and give impetus to his thoughts. He raised his right arm to elbow-angle and swung it to and fro like the pendulum of a clock as he spoke.

"Yessir, all mine joined," he declared. "I had that one there that's never worked a day in the mill to sign a card. I think it's the thing to do. If I was arunnin' the union I'd try to sign up all the new crop out there waitin' for jobs in the mill. Then, when the companies got ready to turn off union members workin' for 'em they couldn't find no non-union ones to take their places.

"They work — the comp'ny, I'm speakin' of — to keep a extry supply of help on hand out here in the village, folks that's been settin' around waitin' for a job like a dog waits for a bone. That away they can hold a threat always over yore head so's to drive you to the last breath and then if you can't do quite as well as they want you to, they can say, 'Git out, you can't keep up, we're done with you, and we've got a dozen that ain't wore out atall out there waitin' and abawlin' for yore job.' That's the reason they take in folks for miles around that's livin' out on farms and glad to get what extry money they can make in the mill. Yessir, they invite 'em in from far and near and they've got folks livin' next door to the mill in comp'ny houses that'd might nigh give part of their life for a job. They's young folks that's never had a job been awaitin' and abeggin' for years to get on down there. And it takes all able-bodied hands in a family aworkin' on the wages they pay to give theirselves a decent livin'. Boys and girls aloafin' — time on their hands to do nothin' with but get in trouble — and no money except what they have to take from them that's not able to give it.

"A farmer out raisin' his stuff and ownin' his land can afford to work twenty-five cent on the dollar cheaper than reg'lar mill people. And the best part for the comp'ny too, he don't need to mutter and grumble and he goes around givin' 'em a good name because so much extry is just so much extry. And families that's helped the comp'ny make what they've got set here in the village with half of 'em waitin' for the word to come to work. Yessir, have 'em so glad to get a job they'll take anything for pay."

The pause was transitory. George's hand was poised in mid-air. Hannah leaned over from her space on the side of the bed, caught her father's hand, and in a sing-song voice declared, "Pa's a preacher, Pa's a preacher."

All of the family laughed with unrestrained glee. The little boy who had cried clapped his hands to give expression to his great good feeling. Hannah beamed over the success of her joke.

"Like back in '32," George was saying, his arm beating in clocklike rhythm, "I come home and found five jobless men settin' on my porch. Five that couldn't to save their lives find a lick of work to do. One of 'em was Clem Martin and I'd knowed Clem ever since I'd been in New Falls. He says to me when I stepped up on the porch, 'Well, George, I wish I was lucky as you, had a good job to go to of a mornin'.' I says, 'Well Clem, I'm thankful I've got a job to go to but it ain't what you'd call a real good job, I don't suppose. I don't draw but two dollars and five cent for a pretty worrisome piece of work.' He says, 'George, if I knowed that you'd quit the job and wasn't goin' to have it back noway nor nohow I'd go right straight down there and ask for it and if the boss said, 'You can have it if you'll work for a dollar a day,' I'd be so thankful at gettin' it atall I ain't certain I wouldn't cry right there and I've never cried but once since I've been a man.'

"Yessir, I think when a comp'ny like this owns a village they ought to be made by law to give a job to every able-bodied man and woman living in it and wantin' to work before they'd be allowed to bring in help from the outside. And I wish I could live to see the union sign up all the workin'-age boys and girls as well as the ones in the mill and I believe the workin' man would get a fairer deal."

"Did many of the people here join the union during the strike?" I asked.

"Lots of 'em joined but most is scared to tell it," George replied.

The girls laughed and exchanged glances among themselves. Mary said, "Maybe we oughtn't to be tellin'. But, law, I've showed my card to more'n one."

"They can't turn you off," Louise declared. "The new law gives a person the right to join the union. Taint like it was after the tater patch meetins."

"Now them was pitiful times for some," George said. "They come a man here back in '31 to hold union meetins and wouldn't none let him have a buildin' to hold 'em in. You see, the man that owns these mills near 'bout controls the whole city and he coulder ruint any man that rented his buildin'. But they went out yonder on the edge of town in a open field and a good many attended. Some joined. Now one way or another the company got word of ever one that joined and they give 'em ten-day notice. Some wouldn't move. The law come out and moved they things to the street.

"The next Sunday evenin' me and old man Tunney rode around Rimmerton where the worst was goin' on, and on two streets we counted eleven families settin' out on the sidewalk beside their things. To see them little children settin' out there with no manner of shelter over their heads, to see the women wore out with tryin' to live, sure put you to thinkin' and made you sorry you had to stop at thinkin'. What you thought about the ones that would do it wouldn't make no pleasant talk. It ain't no wonder folks here is still scared of the union.

"It looked for a while like them folks wasn't goin' to move off the streets. Up town they couldn't seem to figger out the law on it, but finally they got the health doctor to come out and declare the right sanitation wan't bein' carried out. He called their way of livin' a menace to public health and they moved 'em som'ers, I never did know where."

Ruth's eyes were like a flame as she spoke. "I'll stick by the union if it'll try to get me a decent wage for my work so's I can raise my children. I work like a dog in the spinnin' room and when I'm lucky enough to get four days I do as much or more as used to be done in five and a half but I'm paid about like what I ought to make in three.

"When they first put in that new Long Draft machinery women down there fainted and fell out. I fainted once myself. When I come to, my bossman was standin' over me and I was so scared of him I fainted again."

The picture of the second fainting drew laughter from the crowd. Its spirit still lingered in the room when the door was opened after a light rap upon it and a man walked in. He nodded at the crowd, leaned against the wall, and looked at the twins. "I've come to collect," he said. "We've got nothin' for you this week," Mary replied. "We can't even pay Mama our reg'lar board. We'll pay next week." "Don't pay to get behind with your insurance," the young man said. "I know but we can't help it," Louise said.

The young man turned and looked at me. "Selling insurance too?" he asked.

"No, but I feel very much at home with insurance people," I replied. "I usually meet one or two in most mill village homes I visit if it happens to be pay day."

"They're the hanginest round folks you ever seen," Mrs. McBane declared. "Before you can get a bite of bread in your mouth," she continued, raising her fat arm toward her mouth and stopping just short of reaching it, "they're at your door knock, knock." She concluded with imaginary raps in the air.

The insurance man grinned sheepishly and pushed his hat to the back of his head. "Well, insurance is a pretty good thing to have, Mrs. McBane," he said finally.

"I'll never be without it long as I can drag and make a dollar," Ruth declared. "I seen what it meant to have somebody you loved dead and waitin' to be buried and not a penny to your name to bury 'em with. If I can help it the welfare won't have to bury me and the children. I may have to do without things I need to eat but I'll have money laid back in insurance for my folks to buy a coffin to bury me in when I'm dead."

Mrs. McBane broke the silence. "I reckin that there insurance man has seen as many little new-born babies as air doctor in New Falls. He's there to write 'em up before they've let out their first yell."

A roar of laughter went around the room and was sustained by a belated cackle from George who seemingly had thought upon the words before he allowed them to provoke him to laughter.

Presently the young man made his departure but first he warned the twins to have his money ready the next pay day. He tempered the caustic tone of his demand by smiling as he went out of the door.

A restlessness invaded the room which could not immediately resolve itself into conversation. Bodies shifted, feet shuffled. Presently Mary as if moved by a sudden inspiration jumped to her feet, went into the kitchen and came back with a pan of water and a cake of soap. She placed the water on the stove, reached up on the closet door, secured the big washcloth hanging there, and dipped it into the small pan. She soaped the rag with a great display of energy, and began to give her face a vigorous scrubbing.

"You talk about bein' strict," Louise said after awhile, "if you had to inspect in the clothroom under our supervisor you'd think you was in school with the meanest teacher in the United States standin' over you. She has a fit if we so much as open our mouths. For eight hours we go as hard as we can pedalling the machine while the cloth runs through, strainin' our eyes to find a little bad place in it, and if we have three cuts out of the two or three hundred we do a day to come back on us she sends us out to rest the next day. It's her way of punishin' us. The other day two girls had went over to the fountain to get a drink of water — most of us run there and back so's not to be fussed at for leavin' our work — and a man they knowed passed by and spoke to 'em. They wasn't gone no time but a little longer'n usual, so the supervisor sent 'em home and told 'em they'd better rest a day and then maybe they could stay at their work. They know how bad we hate to miss time when don't none of us make enough to get along on anyhow."

Mary emerged shortly from behind the folds of the big washcloth, her face a glowing red. She went into the kitchen to empty the pan and returned with fresh water for Louise. "I think your face needs washin' too," she said to her, and instantly the other twin was engaged in soaping the rag for a face scrubbing. Her face was well covered in lather when someone tapped on the door and Mary tripped across the room to open it. A woman past middle age who carried a big black satchel in her hands came in. "Have this here seat, Mrs. Flack," George said, rising and placing his chair near the center of the room. Mrs. Flack seated herself and lost no time in opening up her satchel and drawing forth brightly colored dish towels. "These," she said to Sally, "are to be give away to everyone taking a $1.00 order this week. It's a very attractive offer. Wouldn't you like a little flavoring set this time, Mrs. Dobbin?"

"I'm afraid I can't take nothin' this time, Mrs. Flack," Sally replied. "The twins lost time last week and I'm shorter'n usual on money."

"And I've no longer got a job," George said, but Mrs. Flack did not seem to hear him.

"You don't have to pay me today," she said to Sally.

"I don't believe I'll take it," Sally said. "I don't won't to get no further in debt. 'Twon't be nothin' for me this week, Mrs. Flack. Ruth has took all that cough medicine she got from you but that little bit up there in the bottle, but it ain't seemed to do her no good atall."

Mrs. Flack raised her eyes to the mantel to look at the almost empty bottle. "It is nearly gone," she said. "Better let me leave you another bottle."

"No, I reckin not this time," Sally responded.

After unsuccessful efforts to supply the twins with vanishing cream Mrs. Flack closed her bag and departed, promising as she did so to return at an early date.

"That Garbo-Christian line's right good," Sally said when the door had closed, "but it comes pretty high."

George grabbed his chair, restored it to its former place, and speaking as a man who has discovered a truth he must express, he said, "Now cuttin' the hours ain't cut down on the joblessness atall. I believe it has actually increased it.

"What the manufacturer done was to stretch the stretchout a little more and speed up the machinery so's to get the same production with less help and shorter time. The mills is makin' the same amount of goods in three and four days as they used to make in a full week. Anybody'll tell you that.

"Twenty-four looms is aplenty for any person to run. Most runs thirty-two. Thirty-six batteries is enough for any young boy or girl to fill — takes 'em young on that job, old ones couldn't keep up — and they've got forty-eight apiece. The cardroom man used to run two slubbers and now they've give him three. When I come here it took seventeen men to keep up with the quill job; now the same work is bein' done by nine. They used to be a tangle man but now if you was to catch up five minutes with your own job the bossman says, 'Get over there and start to untanglin'.' First one and then another works at it till it gets done.[12]

"What they really need is a committee of men that knows mill work from beginnin' to end — men hired by the governmint and not the comp'ny you understand — to go around and say, 'Now twenty-four looms is a fair job, so many batteries is enough for one person to fill,' and like that right on down to the sweeper. It's the work and not the hours that's needin' governmint regulation.

"I do think that Roosevelt is the biggest-hearted man we ever had in the White House. He undoubtedly is the most foresighted and can speak his thoughts the plainest of any man I ever heard speak. He's spoke very few words over the radio that I haven't listened to. It's the first time in my ricollection that a president ever got up and said, 'I'm interested in and aim to do somethin' for the workin' man.' Just knowin' that for once in the time of the country they was a man to stand up and speak for him, a man that could make what he felt so plain nobody could doubt he meant it, has made a lot of us feel a sight better even when they wasn't much to eat in our homes.

---

[12] This paragraph explains, in technical terms, the central labor issue in southern textiles in the 1930s: the unilateral increases in work assignments known to workers as the *stretchout*. Weavers saw increases in the number of looms they had to tend, as did the workers who filled the loom *batteries* (a battery was a device that fed full bobbins of yarn to shuttles when the old bobbins were exhausted). The *cardroom* was the room where the raw cotton was cleaned, the fibers laid parallel to each other in a sheet, and further shaped into a rope prior to spinning; the *slubber* was one of the machines used in this preparatory stage. *Quilling* was the process of transferring yarn to the bobbins, or *quills*, used in the shuttles; if yarn got tangled in the process, a *tangle man* was once employed to clean it up, but that task was now added to that of other workers.

"Roosevelt picked us up out of the mud and stood us up but whenever he turns us loose I'm afraid we're goin' to fall and go deeper in the mud than we was before. That's because so many of his own party has turned against him and brought defeat to lots of his thinkin' and plannin'. The Bible says, 'A house divided against itself cannot stand, a kingdom divided against itself will end in desolation.' If they keep abuckin' against him and bigheads get in there that try to make too quick a turn back, desolation will follow in our country.

"Roosevelt is the only president we ever had that thought the Constitution belonged to the pore man too. The way they've been areadin' it it seemed like they thought it said, 'Him that's got money shall have the rights to life, freedom and happiness.' Is they any freedom to bein' throwed out of yore home and have to watch yore children suffer just because you joined a organization you thought might better you? Does it make you think you've got liberty to be treated like that when the man you're workin' for has always had the right to join the association to multiply his own good livin'? Yessir, it took Roosevelt to read in the Constitution and find out them folks way back yonder that made it was talkin' about the pore man right along with the rich one. I am a Roosevelt man."

George Dobbin's children had listened absorbedly to his solemn pronouncements. They gave the impression once he had finished of persons who had had their own thoughts spoken for them. They were beyond the ties of family bound together now in the unity of common thought. There was no immediate need for continued speech or action and the silence which followed was restful and full of ease.

Presently a bright-faced boy of perhaps thirteen came into the room and Sally introduced him as her youngest child, Henry. "He's the only one I've got in school now," she added. "He's in the eighth grade. How come you so late, Henry?"

"I went by the Y awhile," the boy answered as he passed into the kitchen. There came into the room the sound of one plate being slipped from a stack of plates followed by the click of a stove door opening.

Mary in deep preoccupation cast a critical glance from first one member of her family to the other. "Why, Henry's already gone farther in school than any of us," she said finally. The thought amused her and she laughed. All the younger Dobbins joined her.

"None the rest of us ever got past the seventh grade, did we?" Louise said. "Dan, he was so busy totin' us younguns around he didn't get that far. Mama used to say she bet Dan had rolled me and Mary as far as from here to New York and back in that double baby carriage we had."

"They was a woman in Henderson," Sally began, "that had twins too but hers died. She heard about mine and sent word to me she'd sell their carriage to me for four dollars. Then I was considered one of the best hands in Henderson for doin' up bonnets. I done enough bonnets to buy the carriage and I don't see to save my life how I'der raised them twins without it.

"Mary, they's somebody else aknockin' on the door. It'll about be Mr. Hunter comin' for a paymint on my dress."

Mary came back presently followed by a fat, well-dressed man who after a general nod at the crowd directed his attention toward Sally. "How are you, Mrs. Dobbin," he said, and Sally, reaching into her pocket answered, "All right, I reckin, Mr. Hunter. Here's your fifty cent and I'll try to have the rest of it next week." "That's all right, Mrs. Dobbin," Mr. Hunter answered, and after a smile to all left the room.

"He's a dress peddler," Sally explained, "and a mighty nice man. Him and his brother runs a store up town and he puts part of the goods in his car and comes around peddlin' 'em out. Some times the children fusses at me for buyin' from him because they say his wash dresses is always about fifty cent higher than they are up town but he's so nice about waitin' for his money. Sometimes a body may be able to save fifty cent a week to pay on a dress when they can't save a dollar and a half at a time to buy one. I appreciate how nice Mr. Hunter is about waitin'.".

I looked out of the window and already the foggy day was losing the little of its light that remained. I arose to leave and after I had said good-bye to the crowd Sally got up and accompanied me to the door. I was going down the porch steps when someone called my name. I turned around and George Dobbin stood there just outside of the door, and by the light from the nearby street light I could see the solemn expression on his face.

"If ever you get to talk to any that it'll do any good to talk to," he said, "they's one law you might tell 'em oughter be passed. It is a sin and a shame for air comp'ny in the world to run a elevator without a reg'lar operator. It's my ricollection I've never heard tell of a accident on a elevator where they was a reg'lar operator. But many a time I've read where folks has gone to a horrible death when they've got on one and never knowed how to run it.

"Course if this comp'ny was to get a reg'lar man for the job it'd more'n likely not be me. I'm old and they don't want me. But the law ought really to be passed.

"No, I don't know as I'll ever have another mill job," he muttered as he turned to go back into the house.

Quantitative: Statistical Evidence from Odum's *Southern Regions*

While eyewitness accounts such as those presented in the first chapter of Part Three offer powerful insights into the impact of southern poverty on those trapped in it, the *Report* was made possible by the systematic gathering, compilation, and analysis of data. As noted in Part One, the greatest compendium of such data available to the *Report's* authors was Howard W. Odum's *Southern Regions of the United States* (1936). This chapter provides a selection of tables and maps from Odum's book, with the object of showing how concerned southerners and others came to understand the region's problems, not as a collection of life stories but as a pattern of interrelated pathologies defining the entire South as a "problem" crying out for solution. Tables 1 and 2 and Figure 6 show how southern per capita incomes and farm incomes lagged behind those of the rest of the nation even before 1920. Table 3, with statistics on the extent of soil erosion, illustrates Gerald W. Johnson's point about the South as a "wasted land." Table 4, showing the extent of child and female labor in the region, suggests other, human, forms of waste, and illustrates some of the concerns of northern workers with southern competition. Table 5 and Figure 7, showing illiteracy rates, reveal some of the consequences of underdevelopment for the region's "human capital" endowment and also demonstrate the much greater disabilities suffered by southern blacks. Finally, the four county maps of Mississippi in Figure 8 show the paradoxical association of major cotton-growing areas (with their cotton-derived wealth) with high rates of tenancy and poor diet. What do you think is going on here?

Table 1. Per Capita Personal Income, by Geographic Divisions and States, 1929

STATE AND REGION	ENTIRE POPULATION	NON-FARM POPULATION	FARM POPULATION
Southeast	**$365**	**$535**	**$183**
Virginia	431	594	182
North Carolina	317	472	167
South Carolina	261	412	129
Georgia	343	532	147
Florida	548	577	419
Kentucky	398	605	148
Tennessee	346	529	137
Alabama	331	527	141
Mississippi	287	530	173
Arkansas	311	503	185
Louisiana	438	603	186
Southwest	**564**	**683**	**366**
Oklahoma	503	699	243
Texas	531	690	298
New Mexico	476	549	354
Arizona	744	795	567
Northeast	**881**	**946**	**366**
Maine	645	689	474
New Hampshire	652	689	379
Vermont	633	761	351
Massachusetts	975	976	898
Rhode Island	881	881	859
Connecticut	1,008	1,028	630
New York	1,365	1,417	493
New Jersey	1,002	1,011	704
Delaware	1,315	1,550	368
Pennsylvania	815	865	305
Maryland	799	881	323
West Virginia	485	602	157
Middle States	**715**	**854**	**262**
Ohio	795	893	255
Indiana	614	748	221
Illinois	987	1,091	299
Michigan	869	983	283
Wisconsin	682	807	389
Minnesota	610	802	248
Iowa	485	659	214
Missouri	675	851	189
Northwest	**590**	**703**	**426**
North Dakota	422	588	302
South Dakota	420	614	268
Nebraska	521	698	281
Kansas	569	686	376
Montana	698	856	435
Idaho	609	647	559
Wyoming	777	841	648
Colorado	690	772	470
Utah	600	629	496
Far West	**921**	**953**	**818**
Nevada	1,000	1,041	811
Washington	841	887	651
Oregon	757	817	563
California	1,085	1,066	1,246

119

Table 2.   Farm Income, Five, and Ten-Year Average[a] (See Figure 6, page 126)

STATE	RANK	FIVE-YEAR AVERAGE GROSS INCOME 1924–1928	RANK	FIVE-YEAR AVERAGE GROSS CROP INCOME 1924–1928	RANK	TEN-YEAR AVERAGE[b] CASH FARM INCOME 1920–1921 1930–1931
Arizona	1	$5,260	2	$2,825	3	$3,519
Nevada	2	5,130	33	759	2	3,861
California	3	4,360	1	3,035	1	4,235
New Jersey	4	3,550	4	2,038	6	2,814
North Dakota	5	3,420	3	2,319	9	2,492
Wyoming	6	3,310	27	859	7	2,621
Nebraska	7	3,360	17	1,055	5	2,856
Iowa	8	3,310	36	662	4	3,048
Montana	9	3,080	5	1,614	14	2,317
South Dakota	10	2,940	24	955	10	2,486
Idaho	11	2,920	7	1,589	13	2,332
Kansas	12	2,700	11	1,272	12	2,388
Colorado	12	2,700	10	1,326	11	2,424
Illinois	14	2,650	16	1,086	16	2,237
Washington	15	2,560	6	1,590	8	2,511
Connecticut	16	2,530	15	1,123	15	2,289
Rhode Island	17	2,480	25	885	23	1,988
Utah	18	2,430	23	989	24	1,853
Minnesota	19	2,370	34	725	22	2,016
Oregon	20	2,340	14	1,147	17	2,170
Massachusetts	21	2,250	19	1,042	20	2,072
New York	22	2,270	26	877	18	2,077
Wisconsin	23	2,100	48	443	21	2,072
Delaware	24	2,090	12	1,242	26	1,634
Vermont	25	1,980	41	580	19	2,073
Florida	26	1,940	8	1,569	25	1,665
Maryland	27	1,910	18	1,054	27	1,601
Texas	28	1,830	9	1,341	28	1,594
New Mexico	29	1,780	39	628	35	1,368
Oklahoma	29	1,780	13	1,219	36	1,329
Indiana	31	1,740	42	569	30	1,505
Ohio	32	1,700	40	598	32	1,471
Pennsylvania	33	1,670	37	653	31	1,476
Maine	34	1,610	22	990	29	1,588
Missouri	34	1,610	45	486	37	1,292
Michigan	36	1,570	38	644	33	1,405
New Hampshire	37	1,460	43	543	34	1,396
North Carolina	38	1,310	20	1,034	38	994
Louisiana	39	1,270	21	1,025	49	849
Georgia	40	1,140	29	836	44	677
Virginia	41	1,120	35	697	39	871
Arkansas	42	1,090	31	823	42	749
Mississippi	43	1,050	28	841	48	604
South Carolina	44	1,040	30	826	41	784
West Virginia	45	1,030	46	480	45	674
Alabama	45	1,030	32	785	47	629
Tennessee	47	920	44	541	43	710
Kentucky	48	900	47	461	46	664

[a]Based on crops and Markets, U.S. Department of Agriculture. U.N.C. *News Letter*, Vol. XVI, No. 1.
[b]Adapted by S. H. Hobbs from *Brookmire's Economic Service*, February, 1931, and U.S. Censuses of Agriculture.
Source: Howard W. Odum, *Southern Regions of the United States* (Chapel Hill: University of North Carolina Press, 1936), 20.

Table 3.   Preliminary Estimate of Soil Impoverishment and Destruction by Erosion (Areas in millions of acres)

REGION	APPROXIMATE AREA OF REGION	SEVERELY IMPOVERISHED OR SOIL WASHED OFF	DEVASTATED	TOTAL EROSION	PER CENT
Piedmont	46.0	12.0	4.5	16.5	35.8
Triassic Piedmont	5.0	1.2	0.4	1.6	32.0
Appalachian Mountains	78.0	12.0	3.0	15.0	19.2
Mississippi-Alabama-Georgia Sandy Lands	27.0	6.5	2.0	8.5	31.4
Southern Brown Loam	17.0	4.5	1.8	6.3	37.0
Texas-Arkansas-Louisiana Sandy Lands	33.0	9.5	1.5	11.0	33.3
Texas-Alabama-Mississippi Black Belt	12.0	4.5	1.0	5.5	45.8
Red Plains of Texas, Oklahoma	36.0	15.0	3.0	18.0	50.0
Total	**254.0**	**65.2**	**17.2**	**82.4**	**32.4**
Estimates of other southern areas, e.g., Ozarks, coastal plain[a]	—	10.0	5.0	15.0	—
Grand Total, South	254.0	75.2	22.2	97.4	—
Total for Nation	—	12.5	34.2	159.2	—
Per Cent which South is of Total	—	—	—	—	61.1

[a]The above table except the estimates in this line adapted from H. H. Bennett, *American Geographic Review*, May, 1933.
Source: Howard W. Odum, *Southern Regions of the United States* (Chapel Hill: University of North Carolina Press, 1936), 38.

Table 4. Proportion of Gainfully Occupied, 1930, among the General Population 10 Years and Over, Females 10 Years and Over, and Children 10–17 Years

	GENERAL POPULATION		FEMALES		CHILDREN	
	Number Gainfully Occupied	Per Cent of Total Population 10 Years and Over	Number Gainfully Occupied	Per Cent of Total Females 10 Years and Over	Number Gainfully Occupied	Per Cent of Total Children 10–17 Years
United States	48,829,880	49.4	10,752,076	22.1	2,145,960	11.3
Southeast						
Virginia	880,211	47.0	182,267	19.5	48,641	11.5
North Carolina	1,140,971	48.5	272,965	22.9	111,897	18.6
South Carolina	687,737	53.2	206,761	31.2	92,447	26.3
Georgia	1,162,158	51.9	311,939	27.4	121,408	22.4
Florida	598,939	51.0	149,984	25.7	29,587	13.1
Kentucky	907,095	45.2	146,678	14.8	48,997	11.2
Tennessee	958,386	47.3	195,324	19.1	62,918	14.1
Alabama	1,026,295	51.3	254,014	25.1	116,667	24.0
Mississippi	844,905	55.4	231,728	30.3	111,073	30.5
Arkansas	667,845	47.0	119,193	17.0	57,318	17.1
Louisiana	815,616	50.3	191,420	23.5	59,455	16.6
Total	**9,690,158**	**49.6**	**2,262,273**	**23.0**	**860,408**	**18.8**
Southwest						
Oklahoma	828,004	44.9	129,346	14.5	31,796	7.8
Texas	2,206,767	48.5	421,708	18.9	125,744	13.1
New Mexico	142,607	45.4	22,101	14.7	5,920	8.2
Arizona	165,296	49.3	29,971	19.4	5,595	8.4
Total	**3,342,674**	**47.4**	**603,126**	**17.7**	**169,055**	**11.2**
Northeast						
Maine	308,603	48.0	68,493	21.4	8,141	7.0
New Hampshire	192,666	50.4	49,956	25.9	5,852	8.9
Vermont	141,203	48.4	28,397	19.9	4,494	8.5
Massachusetts	1,814,315	51.7	528,999	29.2	60,524	9.9
Rhode Island	297,172	53.0	87,829	30.4	16,144	15.8
Connecticut	677,208	51.2	178,007	26.8	32,129	12.8
New York	5,523,337	52.5	1,415,105	26.9	174,359	10.2
New Jersey	1,712,106	51.4	416,512	25.1	75,779	12.5
Pennsylvania	3,722,103	48.1	803,892	20.9	156,351	10.1
Delaware	98,104	49.9	20,883	21.6	3,480	9.9
Maryland	672,879	50.8	157,692	23.9	30,656	12.8
D. of Columbia	243,853	58.2	88,825	40.1	3,855	7.3
West Virginia	570,452	43.8	82,198	13.1	20,707	6.9
Total	**15,974,001**	**50.6**	**3,926,788**	**24.9**	**592,471**	**10.4**

Table 4. (*continued*)

	GENERAL POPULATION		FEMALES		CHILDREN	
	Number Gainfully Occupied	Per Cent of Total Population 10 Years and Over	Number Gainfully Occupied	Per Cent of Total Females 10 Years and Over	Number Gainfully Occupied	Per Cent of Total Children 10–17 Years
Middle States						
Ohio	2,615,764	48.1	539,606	20.1	58,097	6.0
Indiana	1,251,065	47.4	235,304	18.1	31,404	6.7
Illinois	3,184,684	50.3	715,468	22.9	95,780	8.8
Michigan	1,927,347	49.5	359,822	19.4	47,967	6.8
Wisconsin	1,129,461	47.5	215,214	18.7	35,183	7.8
Minnesota	992,798	47.8	200,965	19.9	31,145	7.8
Iowa	912,835	45.5	163,522	16.5	28,236	7.6
Missouri	1,457,968	48.9	299,234	20.1	57,606	11.1
Total	**13,471,922**	**48.6**	**2,729,135**	**20.0**	**385,418**	**7.7**
Northwest						
North Dakota	240,303	45.6	36,213	14.8	10,036	8.0
South Dakota	247,653	45.6	37,310	14.6	8,478	7.2
Nebraska	507,008	45.8	89,721	16.7	16,285	7.6
Kansas	694,232	45.7	119,160	16.1	19,407	6.8
Montana	216,479	49.8	32,274	16.7	5,673	6.5
Idaho	162,232	46.5	22,286	13.9	4,624	6.0
Wyoming	92,448	51.7	12,739	16.4	2,288	6.8
Colorado	402,867	48.2	80,993	20.0	13,315	8.5
Utah	170,000	44.0	28,984	15.4	4,938	5.4
Total	**2,733,222**	**46.5**	**459,680**	**16.3**	**85,044**	**7.2**
Far West						
Washington	664,730	50.6	126,676	20.6	12,246	5.5
Oregon	409,645	51.0	81,142	21.3	9,530	7.2
California	2,500,644	52.0	557,354	24.2	31,195	4.6
Nevada	42,884	56.4	5,902	19.3	593	5.3
Total	**3,617,903**	**51.7**	**771,074**	**23.3**	**53,564**	**5.1**

Source: Howard W. Odum, *Southern Regions of the United States* (Chapel Hill: University of North Carolina Press, 1936), 96.

Table 5. Percent Illiteracy Ten Years of Age and Over, 1930 (See Figure 7, page 126)

STATE	TOTAL RANK	TOTAL %	NATIVE WHITE RANK	NATIVE WHITE %	NEGRO RANK	NEGRO %	MALE RANK	MALE %	FEMALE RANK	FEMALE %	21 AND OVER, MALE RANK	21 AND OVER, MALE %	21 AND OVER, FEMALE RANK	21 AND OVER, FEMALE %
Iowa	1	0.8	7	0.4	2	2.0	1	0.8	1	0.7	1	1.0	1	.9
Oregon	2	1.0	32	1.5	5	2.5	2	1.0	2	0.9	3	1.3	2	1.1
Washington	2	1.0	2	0.3	7	2.9	2	1.0	3	1.0	2	1.2	3	1.3
Idaho	4	1.1	7	0.4	17	4.2	6	1.2	3	1.0	6	1.5	3	1.3
South Dakota	5	1.2	7	0.4	4	2.2	4	1.1	9	1.4	4	1.4	9	1.9
Nebraska	5	1.2	7	0.4	13	3.9	4	1.1	6	1.2	4	1.4	7	1.6
Kansas	5	1.2	15	0.5	27	5.9	8	1.3	6	1.2	7	1.6	6	1.5
Utah	5	1.2	2	0.3	10	3.2	8	1.3	5	1.1	9	1.7	5	1.4
Minnesota	9	1.3	7	0.4	2	2.0	6	1.2	8	1.3	7	1.6	8	1.7
North Dakota	10	1.5	7	0.4	11	3.4	10	1.4	11	1.6	10	1.8	13	2.3
Wyoming	11	1.6	2	0.3	17	4.2	11	1.7	11	1.6	11	2.0	11	2.0
Indiana	12	1.7	27	0.9	28	6.0	13	1.8	10	1.5	13	2.3	9	1.9
Montana	12	1.7	2	0.3	21	4.6	11	1.7	13	1.7	12	2.1	13	2.3
Wisconsin	14	1.9	19	0.6	20	4.4	13	1.8	15	1.9	14	2.4	15	2.5
Michigan	15	2.0	22	0.7	8	3.0	15	1.9	17	2.1	14	2.4	17	2.7
Vermont	16	2.2	29	1.3	23	4.9	19	2.6	13	1.7	21	3.2	12	2.2
Missouri	17	2.3	32	1.5	32	8.8	19	2.6	16	2.0	19	3.1	15	2.5
Ohio	17	2.3	22	0.7	30	6.4	16	2.3	19	2.2	16	2.9	19	2.9
Illinois	19	2.4	19	0.6	12	3.6	16	2.3	22	2.6	16	2.9	23	3.3
California	20	2.6	2	0.3	9	3.1	19	2.6	22	2.6	18	3.0	21	3.2
Maine	21	2.7	34	1.6	22	4.8	26	3.2	17	2.1	23	3.9	17	2.7
New Hampshire	21	2.7	25	0.8	13	3.9	22	2.8	21	2.5	22	3.5	21	3.2
Oklahoma	23	2.8	35	1.7	33	9.3	26	3.2	20	2.4	23	3.9	20	3.1
Colorado	23	2.8	25	0.8	13	3.9	18	2.5	24	3.1	19	3.1	24	3.9

STATE	TOTAL		NATIVE WHITE		NEGRO		MALE		FEMALE		21 AND OVER, MALE		21 AND OVER, FEMALE	
	RANK	%	RANK	%	RANK	%	RANK	%	RANK	%	RANK	%	RANK	%
Pennsylvania	25	3.1	19	0.6	17	4.2	23	2.9	25	3.3	23	3.9	25	4.4
Massachusetts	26	3.5	7	0.4	26	5.4	24	3.1	28	3.9	27	4.0	28	5.0
New York	27	3.7	15	0.5	5	2.5	24	3.1	31	4.3	23	3.9	29	5.4
New Jersey	28	3.8	15	0.5	25	5.1	28	3.5	30	4.2	28	4.4	30	5.5
Maryland	28	3.8	29	1.3	36	11.4	30	4.1	26	3.5	29	5.0	25	4.4
Delaware	30	4.0	28	1.2	37	13.2	31	4.2	27	3.8	31	5.2	27	4.9
Nevada	31	4.5	1	0.2	1	1.5	32	4.3	32	4.5	29	5.0	32	5.6
Connecticut	31	4.5	7	0.4	23	4.9	29	3.9	33	5.1	31	5.2	33	6.8
West Virginia	33	4.8	40	3.7	34	11.3	34	5.5	29	4.1	34	7.0	30	5.5
Rhode Island	34	4.9	22	0.7	31	8.1	33	4.4	34	5.4	33	5.8	35	7.0
Kentucky	35	6.6	46	5.7	40	15.4	37	7.7	34	5.4	38	9.3	33	6.8
Arkansas	36	6.8	39	3.5	41	16.1	36	7.4	37	6.2	37	9.2	39	8.2
Texas	36	6.8	31	1.4	38	13.4	35	6.8	39	6.8	35	7.8	38	8.0
Florida	38	7.1	36	1.9	42	18.8	37	7.7	38	6.5	36	8.7	37	7.8
Tennessee	39	7.2	44	5.4	39	14.9	39	8.4	36	6.0	39	10.3	36	7.7
Virginia	40	8.7	40	3.7	34	11.3	41	10.0	40	7.4	41	12.1	40	9.5
Georgia	41	9.4	38	3.3	43	19.9	42	10.6	41	8.3	42	12.5	41	10.9
North Carolina	42	10.0	45	5.6	44	20.6	43	11.2	42	8.9	44	14.2	42	12.0
Arizona	43	10.1	15	0.5	16	4.0	40	9.0	43	11.4	40	10.4	43	13.7
Alabama	44	12.6	42	4.8	47	26.2	45	13.5	44	11.6	46	16.6	44	15.2
Mississippi	45	13.1	37	2.7	45	23.2	47	14.4	45	11.8	47	18.0	45	15.6
New Mexico	46	13.3	48	7.7	28	6.0	43	11.2	48	15.7	43	13.6	48	20.3
Louisiana	47	13.5	47	7.3	46	23.3	46	13.6	46	13.5	45	16.5	46	17.2
South Carolina	48	14.9	43	5.1	48	26.9	48	15.8	47	14.1	48	18.8	47	18.4

Source: Howard W. Odum, *Southern Regions of the United States* (Chapel Hill: University of North Carolina Press, 1936), 104.

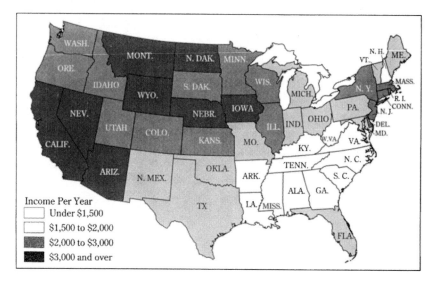

Figure 6.   Average Gross Income per Farm per Year, 1924–1928
Source: Howard W. Odum, *Southern Regions of the United States* (Chapel Hill: University of
North Carolina Press, 1936), 20.

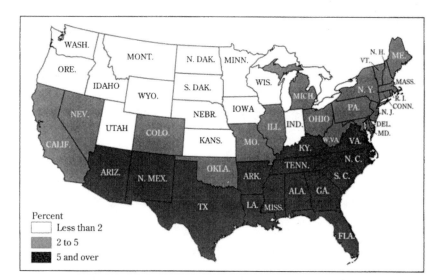

Figure 7.   Percent Total Illiteracy Ten Years of Age and Over, 1930
Source: Adapted from Howard W. Odum, *Southern Regions of the United States* (Chapel Hill:
University of North Carolina Press, 1936), 104.

Figure 8. Cotton Economy in the Mississippi Delta

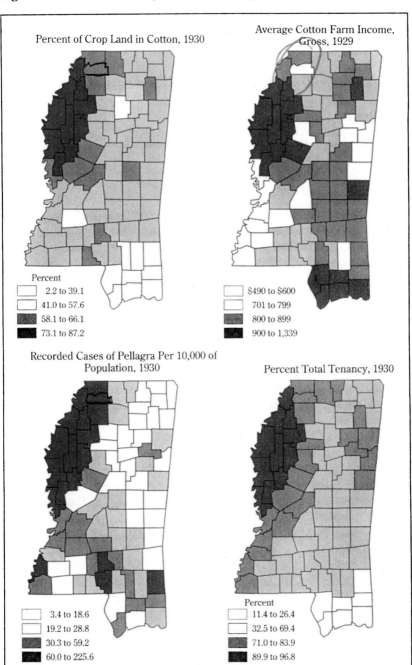

Percent of Crop Land in Cotton, 1930

Average Cotton Farm Income, Gross, 1929

Percent
- ☐ 2.2 to 39.1
- ☐ 41.0 to 57.6
- ▨ 58.1 to 66.1
- ■ 73.1 to 87.2

- ☐ $490 to $600
- ☐ 701 to 799
- ▨ 800 to 899
- ■ 900 to 1,339

Recorded Cases of Pellagra Per 10,000 of Population, 1930

Percent Total Tenancy, 1930

- ☐ 3.4 to 18.6
- ☐ 19.2 to 28.8
- ▨ 30.3 to 59.2
- ■ 60.0 to 225.6

Percent
- ☐ 11.4 to 26.4
- ☐ 32.5 to 69.4
- ▨ 71.0 to 83.9
- ■ 89.9 to 96.8

Source: Howard W. Odum, *Southern Regions of the United States* (Chapel Hill: University of North Carolina Press, 1936), 422.

Contemporary Documents
Relating to the *Report*

The following documents have been chosen to illustrate the history of the *Report,* the ways in which it was used, the controversy it ignited, and the responses it elicited from liberal southerners. The *Report* was intended at least in part as a political document, and Franklin Roosevelt made political use of it in a famous speech delivered at Barnesville, Georgia.

The release of the *Report* stirred enormous controversy, generating a flood of editorial comment. It received a hostile reception from the *Textile Bulletin,* a Charlotte, North Carolina, industrial paper whose editor, David Clark, was noted for his conservatism; on the other hand, its appearance was lauded by the Louisville *Courier-Journal,* a well-regarded liberal paper whose publisher, Barry Bingham, served on the Advisory Council for the *Report.* Note in particular the lessons that the *Courier-Journal's* editorialist drew from the document. The *Report* attracted lengthier critiques as well. Among the most influential was that of Fitz-gerald Hall, a Nashville railroad president and head of the Southern States Industrial Council, an anti–New Deal southern business group; Hall's attack was important enough to require an extended response from Lowell Mellett, the National Emergency Council's director. In the midst of the controversy, southern liberals sought to capitalize on the newfound attention it brought to southern problems to formulate a plan of action. The most important of these efforts was the Southern Conference for Human Welfare held at Birmingham, Alabama, in November 1938. The principal product of this meeting was a set of resolutions, which constitutes our final document. As you read, consider the relationship between these resolutions and the objectives of the *Report* as you understand them. What do the *Report* and these resolutions tell us about the character of southern liberalism of their day?

FRANKLIN D. ROOSEVELT

Using the Report *in the "Purge":*
Speech at Barnesville, Georgia

August 11, 1938

Governor Rivers, Senator George, Senator Russell, and my neighbors of Georgia:

Fourteen years ago a democratic Yankee, a comparatively young man, came to a neighboring county in the State of Georgia, in search of a pool of warm water wherein he might swim his way back to health; and he found it. The place—Warm Springs—was at that time a rather dilapidated small summer resort. His new neighbors there extended to him the hand of genuine hospitality, welcomed him to their firesides and made him feel so much at home that he built himself a house, bought himself a farm, and has been coming back ever since. And he proposes to keep to that good custom. I intend coming back very often.

There was only one discordant note in that first stay of mine at Warm Springs. When the first of the month bill came in for electric light for my little cottage, I found that the charge was eighteen cents per kilowatt hour—about four times as much as I was paying in another community, Hyde Park, New York. That light bill started my long study of proper public utility charges for electric current, started in my mind the whole subject of getting electricity into farm homes throughout the United States.

So, my friends, it can be said with a good deal of truth that a little cottage at Warm Springs, Georgia, was the birthplace of the Rural Electrification Administration. Six years ago, in 1932, there was much talk about the more widespread and cheaper use of electricity; but it is only since March 4, 1933, that your Government has reduced that talk to practical results. Electricity is a modern necessity of life, not a luxury. That necessity ought to be found in every village, in every home, and on every farm in every part of the United States. The dedication of this Rural Electrification Administration project in Georgia today is a symbol of the progress we are making—and we are not going to stop.

Speech at Barnesville, Georgia, August 11, 1938. Franklin D. Roosevelt, *The Public Papers and Addresses of Franklin D. Roosevelt, 1938 Volume* (New York: Macmillan Co., 1941), 463 – 70.

As you know, when I want to go somewhere I generally try to choose the most direct route, but I slipped up this time. I wanted to come to Georgia, but I had to come via California, the Galapagos Islands, the Equator, the Panama Canal, and Pensacola. But, before I left on that trip about a month ago, I invited a group of distinguished, broad-minded Southerners to meet in Washington to discuss the economic conditions and problems of the South. When they met, I said to them:

"My intimate interest in all that concerns the South is, I believe, known to all of you; but this interest is far more than a sentimental attachment born of a considerable residence in your section and of close personal friendship with so many of your people. It proceeds even more from my feeling of responsibility toward the whole Nation. It is my conviction that the South presents right now the Nation's No. 1 economic problem—the Nation's problem, not merely the South's. For we have an economic unbalance in the Nation as a whole, due to this very condition in the South itself.

"It is an unbalance that can and must be righted for the sake of the South and of the Nation."

The day before yesterday when I landed in Florida I received the report and the recommendations based on the advice of this distinguished commission. This report and the recommendations will be made public in the course of the next day or two; and I hope you will read it.

It is well said that this report "presents in only a small degree the manifold assets and advantages possessed by the South" because the report is concerned primarily not with boasting about what the South has, but in telling what the South needs. It is a short report divided into fifteen short sections; and it covers in a broad way subjects of vital importance, such as economic resources, soil, water, population, private and public income, education, health, housing, labor, ownership and use of land, credit, use of natural resources, industry, and purchasing power.

I am listing those fifteen headings with a definite purpose in mind. The very fact that it is necessary to divide the economic needs of the South into fifteen important groups—each one a problem in itself—proves to you and to me that if you and I are to cover the ground effectively, there is no one single simple answer. It is true that many obvious needs ought to be attained quickly—such as the reduction of discriminatory freight rates, such as putting a definite floor under industrial wages, such as continuing to raise the purchasing power of the farm population. But no one of these things alone, no combination of a few of them, will meet the whole of the problem. Talking in fighting terms, we cannot capture one hill and claim to have won the battle, because the battlefront extends over thousands of miles and we must push forward along the whole front at the same time.

That is why the longer I live, the more am I convinced that there are two types of political leadership which are dangerous to the continuation of broad economic and social progress all along that long battlefront. The first type of political leadership which is dangerous to progress is represented by the man who harps on one or two remedies or proposals and claims that these one or two remedies will cure all our ills. The other type of dangerous leadership is represented by the man who says that he is in favor of progress but whose record shows that he hinders or hampers or tries to kill new measures of progress. He is that type of political leader who tells his friends that he does not like this or that or the other detail; and, at the same time, he utterly fails to offer a substitute that is practical or worthwhile.

The task of meeting the economic and social needs of the South, on the broad front that is absolutely necessary, calls for public servants whose hearts are sound, whose heads are sane—whose hands are strong, striving everlastingly to better the lot of their fellowmen.

The report to which I referred is a synopsis—a clear listing of the economic and social problems of the Southland. It suggests the many steps that must be taken to solve the problems.

Some of these steps, it is true, can be taken by state governments, but you will readily realize that action by the states alone, even if such action on the part of many neighboring states could be simultaneous and immediate, would be wholly inadequate. The very good reason for that is that most of these problems involve interstate relationships, relationships not only among the states of this region but also between each and all of these states and the rest of the Nation.

It is not an attack on state sovereignty to point out that this national aspect of all these problems requires action by the Federal Government in Washington. I do not hesitate to say from long experience that during the past five years there has been a closer and more effective peacetime cooperation between the Governors of the forty-eight states and the President of the United States than at any other time in our whole national history.

You are familiar enough with the processes of Government to know that the Chief Executive cannot take action on national or regional problems, unless they have been first translated into Acts of Congress passed by the Senate and the House of Representatives of the United States.

Such action by the Congress, it is equally clear, must be vigorously supported by the Senators and Representatives whose constituents are directly concerned with Southern economics and Southern social needs. Senators and Congressmen who are not wholeheartedly in sympathy with these needs cannot be expected to give them vigorous support.

Translating that into more intimate terms, it means that if the people of the State of Georgia want definite action in the Congress of the United States, they must send to that Congress Senators and Representatives who are willing to stand up and fight night and day for Federal statutes drawn to meet actual needs—not something that serves merely to gloss over the evils of the moment for the time being—but laws with teeth in them which go to the root of the problems; which remove the inequities, raise the standards and, over a period of years, give constant improvement to the conditions of human life in this State.

You, the people of Georgia, in the coming Senatorial primary, for example, have a perfect right to choose any candidate you wish. I do not seek to impair that right, and I am not going to impair that right of the people of this State; but because Georgia has been good enough to call me her adopted son and because for many long years I have regarded Georgia as my "other state," I feel no hesitation in telling you what I would do if I could vote here next month. I am strengthened in that decision to give you my personal opinion of the coming Senatorial primary by the fact that during the past few weeks I have had many requests from distinguished citizens of Georgia—from people high and low—from the Chief Justice of the highest court of Georgia and many others.

Let me preface my statement by saying that I have personally known three of the candidates for the United States Senate for many years. All of them have had legislative or executive experience as Government servants. We may therefore justly consider their records and their public utterances—and we can justly, also, seek to determine for ourselves what is their inward point of view in relationship to present and future problems of government.

It has been pointed out by writers and speakers who do not analyze public questions very deeply that in passing through the State of Kentucky a month ago I gave as a reason for the reelection of Senator Barkley that he had had very long and successful service in the Congress of the United States and that his opponent did not have that experience. In Kentucky, there was no clear-cut issue between a liberal on the one side and a dyed-in-the-wool conservative on the other. Neither of the two principals on his record could be classified as a reactionary; therefore, the criterion of experience, especially that of the Majority Leadership of the Senate of the United States, weighed heavily, and properly, in favor of Senator Barkley.

Here in Georgia, however, my old friend, the senior Senator from this State, cannot possibly in my judgment be classified as belonging to the liberal school of thought—and, therefore, the argument that he has long served in the Senate falls by the wayside. Here in Georgia the issue is a different one from that in Kentucky.

I speak seriously and in the most friendly way in terms of liberal and conservative for the very simple fact that on my shoulders rests a responsibility to the people of the United States. In 1932 and again in 1936 I was chosen Chief Executive with the mandate to seek by definite action to correct many evils of the past and of the present; to work for a wider distribution of national income, to improve the conditions of life, especially among those who need it most and, above all, to use every honest effort to keep America in the van of social and economic progress.

To the Congress of the United States I make recommendations—that is all—in most cases recommendations relating to objectives, leaving it to the Congress to translate the recommendations into law. The majority of the Senate and House have agreed with those objectives, and have worked with me; and I have worked with them to translate those objectives into action. Some have given "lip service" to some of the objectives but have not raised their little fingers actively to attain the objectives themselves. Too often these few have listened to the dictatorship of a small minority of individuals and corporations who oppose the objectives themselves. That is a real dictatorship and one which we have been getting away from slowly but surely during the past five years. As long as I live, you will find me fighting against any kind of dictatorship—especially the kind of dictatorship which has enslaved many of our fellow citizens for more than half a century.

What I am about to say will be no news, to my old friend—and I say it with the utmost sincerity—Senator Walter George. It will be no surprise to him because I have recently had personal correspondence with him; and, as a result of it, he fully knows what my views are.

Let me make it clear that he is, and I hope always will be, my personal friend. He is beyond question, beyond any possible question, a gentleman and a scholar; but there are other gentlemen in the Senate and in the House for whom I have a real affectionate regard, but with whom I differ heartily and sincerely on the principles and policies of how the Government of the United States ought to be run.

For example, I have had an almost lifelong acquaintance and great personal friendship for people like Senator Hale from the State of Maine, for Representative James Wadsworth of New York and for the Minority Leader, Representative Snell. All of these lifelong conservative Republicans are gentlemen and scholars; but they and I learned long ago that our views on public questions were just as wide apart as the North Pole and the South.

Therefore, I repeat that I trust, and am confident, that Senator George and I shall always be good personal friends even though I am impelled to make it clear that on most public questions he and I do not speak the same language.

To carry out my responsibility as President, it is clear that if there is to be success in our Government there ought to be cooperation between members of my own party and myself—cooperation, in other words, within the majority party, between one branch of Government, the Legislative branch, and the head of the other branch, the Executive. That is one of the essentials of a party form of government. It has been going on in this country for nearly a century and a half. The test is not measured, in the case of an individual, by his every vote on every bill—of course not. The test lies rather in the answer to two questions: First, has the record of the candidate shown, while differing perhaps in details, a constant active fighting attitude in favor of the broad objectives of the party and of the Government as they are constituted today; and, secondly, does the candidate really, in his heart, deep down in his heart, believe in those objectives? I regret that in the case of my friend, Senator George, I cannot honestly answer either of these questions in the affirmative.

In the case of another candidate in the State of Georgia for the United States Senate—former Governor Talmadge—I have known him for many years. His attitude toward me and toward other members of the Government in 1935 and in 1936 concerns me not at all. But, in those years and in this year I have read so many of his proposals, so many of his promises, so many of his panaceas, that I am very certain in my own mind that his election would contribute very little to practical progress in government. That is all I can say about him.

The third candidate that I would speak of, United States Attorney Lawrence Camp, I have also known for many years. He has had experience in the State Legislature; he has served as Attorney General of Georgia and for four years; he has made a distinguished record in the United States District Court, his office ranking among the first two in the whole of the United States in the expedition of Federal cases in that Court. I regard him not only as a public servant with successful experience but as a man who honestly believes that many things must be done and done now to improve the economic and social conditions of the country, a man who is willing to fight for these objectives. Fighting ability is of the utmost importance.

Therefore, answering the requests that have come to me from many leading citizens of Georgia that I make my position clear, I have no hesitation in saying that if I were able to vote in the September primaries in this State, I most assuredly should cast my ballot for Lawrence Camp.

In dedicating this important project today, I want to express once more my abiding faith that we as a nation are moving steadily and surely toward a better way of living for all of our people. This electrification project is a symbol of our determination to attain that objective. But it is only one symbol; it is one hill out of ten thousand which must be captured. You and I will never be satisfied until all our economic inequalities are corrected, until every one of us, North, East, West, and South has the opportunity so to live, that his education, his job, and his home will be secure.

In many countries democracy is under attack by those who charge that democracy fails to provide its people with the needs of modern civilization. I do not, you do not, subscribe to that charge. You and I, we, the people of this State and the people of all the states, believe that democracy today is succeeding, but that an absolute necessity for its future success is the fighting spirit of the American people—their insistence that we go forward and not back.

Two Editorials: From the Textile Bulletin *and the* Louisville Courier-Journal

ROOSEVELT APPOINTS A SLUMMING COMMISSION

Ever since the Civil War, there has been an element of people in the North who have regarded themselves as put on earth for the special purpose of regulating the affairs of the benighted citizens of the South.

It has been a mania with some and with others, such as the officials of the National Child Labor Committee, it has been a profitable source of

---

"Roosevelt Appoints a Slumming Commission," *Textile Bulletin,* July 7, 1938, 14 – 15; "The Truth about Dixie," *Louisville Courier-Journal,* August 16, 1938, 6.

revenue because there have always been wealthy but ignorant people who were willing to finance efforts to force Southern people to adopt their own standards of conduct and standards of living.

The Daily Sun of Lewiston, Maine, once very aptly expressed the situation by the following editorial statement:

> The fundamental theory of this Child Labor Amendment is that we people of Maine are such a damned sight better than the people of North Carolina that we are called of the Lord to go get the Federal club and go down and smash North Carolina into our high state of Christian consecration.

We took off our hat to the editor of *The Lewiston Daily Sun* for so accurately and truthfully sizing up the situation, but he should not have limited his observation to the Child Labor Amendment, for it applies to all laws, customs, and habits of the people of the South.

To a large group of people, we are the wilds of the nation and they have a great hankering to take their clubs and drive us down straight and narrow paths into corrals made according to their own standards.

Now Franklin D. Roosevelt, a Northern man, has appointed a slumming commission called a "Conference on Economic Conditions in the South" and has appointed the following as members: Gov. Carl Bailey of Arkansas, Barry Bingham, publisher of the *Louisville* (Ky.) *Courier-Journal;* President Frank Graham of the University of North Carolina; W. B. Gizzell, president of the Oklahoma State University; L. O. Crosby, Mississippi lumber operator; Major Thomas Allen of Memphis, Tenn., water and light district; Gen. John C. Persons, president of the First National Bank of Birmingham, Ala.; J. S. Wannamaker, past president of the American Cotton Association; Carl White, a Texas leader of the American Federation of Labor, and Lucy R. Mason of Atlanta, field worker for the C. I. O.

There are, no doubt, some upon the commission who will be interested in rendering a real service for the people of the South, but there are at least two, Frank P. Graham and Miss Lucy Mason, who, like the fabled billy goat at the meeting of animals, have "already voted."

It is our opinion that Frank Graham and Miss Mason can write their report just as well now as later and that no evidence given at the hearings will make any change in their conclusions. Both are, we believe, personally interested in directing criticisms toward the industries of the South.

Miss Mason has for years persisted in misrepresenting conditions in the South and as the result has been rewarded with a very lucrative C. I. O. job.

The attitude of Frank Graham toward industry was fully disclosed when he voluntarily sought to furnish bond, by wire, for a man who led a flying squadron in an attack which partially demolished a hosiery mill and drove from that mill those workers who chose to remain at work.[1]

We are firmly convinced that, as far as Mr. Graham and Miss Mason are concerned, the Conference on Economic Conditions in the South will be but an opportunity to express preconceived views and give further publicity to their attacks upon industry.

No patriotic or sensible man would oppose any sincere effort to improve the economic condition of the South, but having walked many times through the densely crowded slum districts of New York City, we are opposed to a man who lives just north of that section singling out the South and appoint[ing] a slumming commission composed partly, at least, of persons who will use the opportunity to make an attack upon those whom they do not like.

The basic problem of the South is the low income of the farm population and when that rises, the industrial income and the prosperity of the South will also rise.

The greatest single thing which could be done to raise the farm income would be to place a tariff upon jute and jute products,[2] and permit cotton to be purchased for the purposes for which jute is now utilized but that would cause the people of the North to pay more for bags and coverings and no such tariff will be placed.

The Manufacturers' Record of Baltimore says about our benighted section which has now been selected for a slumming tour:

> The South as a field for enterprise has advanced during the years of depression in contrast with declines in other sections. Opportunities in this territory for development based upon raw materials which are in

[1] The General Textile Strike of September 1934, the largest strike in American history to that time, involved many thousands of southern textile workers and forced the closing of hundreds of mills. Not all the mills closed, however; to broaden the coverage of the strike, motorized processions, dubbed "flying squadrons," moved from mill to mill seeking their shutdowns, often producing violent confrontations with managers, deputies, national guardsmen, and even other workers. At one such clash, in High Point, North Carolina, a young Socialist Party official and strike sympathizer named Alton Lawrence was arrested on charges of having incited a riot. Graham, who had known Lawrence as a student at the University of North Carolina, immediately asserted his innocence and offered to help pay his bond. Industrialists were incensed at what they regarded as Graham's condoning of mob violence; his defenders countered that he was motivated solely by paternal concern for, and trust in, one of "his boys," and that Lawrence, far from inciting the workers, had sought to calm them. The charges against Lawrence were subsequently dropped, but David Clark, the *Textile Bulletin*'s editor, a man with long-standing antipathy toward Graham, continued to consider them valid.

[2] Jute is an imported fiber widely used in coarse bagging (seed bags, cotton baling, etc.). A tariff on jute and jute products would improve the competitive position of cotton textiles for use as bagging and expand the industrial market for southern cotton, raising farm prices as well. Of course, it would also raise the price of bagging.

abundance are claiming the attention of producers in other parts of the country as never before. . . . There is being developed today [a] frontier of varied opportunities.

The people of the South are capable of handling the problems of the South.

THE TRUTH ABOUT DIXIE

The report of the National Emergency Council on economic conditions in the South addresses itself to the consideration of the people in other sections, not for the appeal to their altruism but to their own larger self-interest.

"The South," says the report, "is the Nation's greatest untapped market and the market in which American business can expand most easily. Northern producers and distributors are losing profits and Northern workers are losing work because the South cannot afford to buy their goods."

They have been regarding the South with a jealous eye for their own safety against a potential competitor, although the industrial development of other sections has expanded, not restricted, the commerce of already developed manufacturing centers.

And here is another item of the report, not entirely unrelated. "A large proportion of the South's natural resources are owned by outside interests. Much of its business and industry" is under the "control of investors from wealthier sections. . . . Child labor is more common in the South than in any other section of the Nation. Moreover, women and children work under fewer legal safeguards than women and children elsewhere." That fixes the blame while it describes the condition. A Southern bloc in Congress represents outside financial interests which are exploiting woman and child labor.

That is what *The Courier-Journal* long ago told the South. It is suffering from cheap labor, a partial burden on local charity, the profit of which it doesn't share. The benefit of industry to a community is measured by the payroll. The smoke adds nothing to its wealth, beauty, health, or culture.

Drawn exclusively by Southern members of the Council with the assistance of an advisory committee of representative Southerners, the report will escape the antagonism which objective criticism frequently incurs as slanderous, and it ought to elevate the thinking in other parts of the country to a more intelligent level. . . .

FITZGERALD HALL AND LOWELL MELLETT

Attack and Response:
Hall's Comments and Mellett's Response

COMMENTS ON THE REPORT
OF ECONOMIC CONDITIONS
OF THE SOUTH

While it is true that the *Report on Economic Conditions of the South* is concerned primarily with what the South needs—and it is conceded that its needs are great—yet in reading the Report one is amazed to find that it deals largely in generalities such as might be applied to almost any other section of the United States with a similar concentration of population, degree of urbanization, and diversification of industry. To the average reader, many of the statements will be ambiguous and misleading, and throughout there seems to be a lack of understanding or ability to evaluate those factors responsible for the economic conditions described. Its inaccuracies, which in general are caused as much by omissions and lack of qualification of statements as anything else, and its sweeping generalities place it in a class with that vast volume of material which has been written about the South deploring its sad state of affairs, holding it up to ridicule and shame, but offering no tangible solution of its problems. It does the South a grave injustice.

Many of us operating businesses in the South, familiar with its actual conditions, consider the South to be the number one economic hope of the Nation.

1. For example, the study is replete with illustrations placing the South in the lower brackets in practically all measures of economic condition, but nowhere is there specific mention made of the depressing influence, in dealing in averages, of the fact that 29 percent of its population is colored. The report does not point out that the standard of living and the income of Negroes everywhere in the United States, in general,

Fitzgerald Hall, "Comments on the Report of [sic] Economic Conditions of the South," September 7, 1938. Frank Porter Graham Papers, Southern Historical Collection, The Library of the University of North Carolina at Chapel Hill, Series 1.1, 1938, folder 70. Lowell Mellett to Fitzgerald Hall, September 19, 1938. Frank Porter Graham Papers, Southern Historical Collection, The Library of the University of North Carolina at Chapel Hill, Series 1.1, 1938, folder 71. This letter was released to newspapers by request.

is lower than that of the white population; nor does it say that with such a large concentration of Negroes in the South average figures for that section are obviously greatly affected thereby.

Why were not the facts brought out which were made available in recent studies of Consumer Purchases by the United States Department of Agriculture, giving a comparison of family income by occupations in 140 villages in the United States? In these studies it was found that the median annual income of nonrelief white families was more in the Southeast than in most other sections of the country. In 15 Georgia and South Carolina villages the annual income was $1,309, in 18 North Carolina and Mississippi villages it was $1,764, as compared with $1,447 for 14 Vermont and Massachusetts villages, $1,075 for 19 Illinois and Iowa villages, $1,167 for 13 villages in Pennsylvania and Ohio, and $1,208 for 14 villages in Michigan and Wisconsin.

However, if Negro families were included, the average for southern villages would be greatly depressed, as compared with the average income in villages that have little or no Negro population. The question might be asked, Why does not the South do something about raising the standards for the Negroes? That problem is nationwide, for the relative economic position of the race is the same in every section of the country, but is simply more noticeable in the South, because of its predominance here. That all should cooperate to alleviate this situation is obvious.

2. Another interesting point brought out in the studies mentioned above is that in the Southeast, North Central, and Middle Atlantic regions, it was possible for families to show increases in net worth on a lower annual wage than in other sections. In other words, proportionately more families showed increases in *net worth* on incomes of from $750 [to] $999 annually in these areas than in other sections. But, this was not brought out in the report. Instead, it was stated that there is little difference in living costs, about 5 percent, as between large cities in the North and South, and this was assumed to apply to the whole South, both rural and urban.

3. In a brief appraisal of the report it is possible to call attention to only a few salient points that need immediate clarification and correction. Among these is the statement on page [64] which says that: "In spite of longer working hours, the total annual wages show the same discrepancies." A report by the Bureau of Labor Statistics covering data for 59 manufacturing industries for 1935 reveals that the average hours worked per month in the South were 152.7 as compared with 159.0 for the North and 165.4 for the West. Figures for April 1938 from the Bureau of Labor

Statistics indicate that the average hours worked for the country as a whole in all manufacturing industries were 34.2 hours per week. In comparison, all manufacturing industries in the South in April averaged 33.8 hours, according to the records of the Southern States Industrial Council; thus refuting the statement that working hours are longer in the South than in other sections.

4. The statement is also made that: "Industrial earnings of workers are often 30 to 50 percent below national averages." A very complete study by the Bureau of Labor Statistics, entitled "Geographical Variation in Hours and Wages during 1933 and 1935," covering 59 selected industries of outstanding importance, points out that: "Some form of [weighting] is also needed to eliminate from the average, as far as possible, differences in hourly earnings that arise from differences in the relative importance of the industries in the several regions." By constructing such a weighted average, it was discovered that industrial wages in the South as a whole, covering industries employing the majority of workers, were only 15.3 percent lower than in the North, although somewhat greater variations were apparent in a few industries. It is also true that there are variations as between sections in the South, but the same thing is true in the North as well. For example, it was found that average wages in the 59 industries in the study referred to above, varied from an average of 49.9¢ in New England states to a high of 66.5¢ in the East North Central states—a difference of 16.6¢, or a differential as between sections in the North of 25 percent. The rate for the South for these same industries was 44.2¢; thus, there is a difference of only 5.7¢ between wages in the South and those in the New England area.

5. The chapter on Industry beginning on page [75] refers to the cotton textile industry and states that: "During the year 1933 the percentage of the wages to the value added by manufacture was 60.8 percent in five States in New England, as against 55.5 percent in five Southern States." It neglects to say, however, that in 1935 wages paid by all southern manufacturers constituted 41.2 percent of the value added by manufacture, while in the North and East wages constituted only 39.4 percent of the value added. Southern manufacturers, after paying wages, salaries, cost of materials, coal, electricity, and ordinary operating expenses, had left, on the average, for each worker employed, with which to pay business overhead such as interest on borrowed money, depreciation, taxes, and dividends, $963.00. In the North that figure was $1,344 per worker. Also in 1935, we find, based upon official records, that the net income of Northern manufacturers was 4.4 percent of the total sales value of their products, as compared with 3.4 percent for Southern manu-

facturers. Comparing wages with profits, the South is more generous to labor than the North.

6. The statement is also made on page [66] that: "The South leads the Nation in the employment of children in both farm and industrial work." This statement is decidedly misleading, for the South does not lead the nation in the employment of children in industrial work. It is a fact that in the New England and Middle Atlantic states, eight out of every thousand children were employed in manufacturing industries in 1930, while in the South, less than six out of every thousand were employed in manufacturing industries. Also, according to the Census figures for 1930, which are the same as those quoted in the report, it is a fact that of all the children employed in the New England and Middle Atlantic States, 41.6 percent were employed in the factories of those sections, while only 5.4 percent of all the children employed in the South were confined within the walls of factories. Conversely, 85.1 percent of all the children employed in the South, were in agriculture, employed for seasonal periods in the year, while in the Northern states designated, only 10.7 percent were thus engaged.

7. A wholly disinterested reader of Section 14, beginning on page [75] of the Report, might well be amazed that any kind of industry in the South could continue to exist if it needed to ship its products into Northern markets. The Southern manufacturer is said to have a 39 percent handicap in reaching those markets as compared with his competitor located in the North. And "the southwestern manufacturer, with a 75 percent relative disadvantage, is even worse off."

If these were the facts, then the economic problem of the South indeed might be desperate. However, it is not a fact that "the southeastern manufacturer sending goods across the boundary into this (northeastern) region is at a relative disadvantage of approximately 39 percent in the charges which he has to pay as compared with the rates for similar shipments entirely within the eastern rate territory." Nor is it true that the southwestern manufacturer has a 75 percent disadvantage. Both do pay more than the charges within eastern territory, but how much more requires inquiry into each specific rate adjustment.

It is variously estimated that the general level of southern rates ranges from 10 percent to 20 percent higher than in the North. In the Canned Goods case, 179 I.C.C. 77, Mr. Commissioner Lee, dissenting, with the concurrence of Mr. Commissioner Tate, said at page 100,

A more nearly correct relationship . . . would make the southern rates approximately 16 per cent higher than within the North. It is my considered opinion that the record utterly fails to justify a greater difference in the rates in the two territories.

In the Furniture Case, 177 I.C.C. 5, the Commission prescribed third class from the South to the North and second class in the North, representing a handicap of about 8 percent against the South. In the Coke Case (various citations), the northern producers contended that the coke rates from the South to the North should be 10 percent higher than within the North, because that seemed to them to express the general difference in other rate cases involving northbound rates. Stove rates are from 15 to 20 percent higher. These differences are severe enough to represent a distinct advantage to producers in northern territory. The South is justified in seeking to alleviate this existing situation, but it is nothing like as great a handicap as stated in the report.

8. The statement is made on page [74], that, "the fabrication plants which use most of the steel were not constructed in the Birmingham area. The fact that these fabrication plants are outside of the South will make it hard for the South now to find a [ready] market for its steel, even though the pricing system has been changed."

As a matter of fact, the South has a number of large fabricating plants of national prominence in addition to many smaller plants, which have ample facilities for handling the construction needs of this area, and for expanding into other areas where they can compete profitably. (We are distinguishing between "fabricators" and "manufacturers.")

9. It would also appear from this Report that only the South's people need radios, milk, butter, eggs, dresses, and shoes, yet less money was spent by the W.P.A. in 1937 in eleven southern states combined than in the single state of Pennsylvania. With only 38 percent of the population of the South, W.P.A. expenditures in Pennsylvania in 1937 amounted to $214,565,158, as compared with $198,038,507 in these eleven southern states. Is Pennsylvania or the South the Nation's Number One Economic Problem?

RESPONSE TO HALL'S COMMENTS

September 19, 1938

Dear Mr. Hall:

I was pleased to receive your letter concerning the recent report to the President on the economic conditions of the South, as well as the mimeographed copy of your more extensive comments made available to the press.

You may not recall the circumstances under which the report was prepared and disseminated. It was in answer to a suggestion by the President that my office provide him with a statement on the economic conditions or needs of the South. To meet this request, I asked and obtained the services of a number of men in various branches of the Government, all of them Southerners, who might be expected to have knowledge of various phases of the South's economic life and whose loyalty to the South could not be questioned. With access to all statistical information in the possession of the Government, they worked some weeks before presenting their report. I then submitted the report to a group of representative southern citizens and asked them, in effect, to edit it—to test its statements against their experience, common sense, and special knowledge.

The report, as published, was the result. If there are errors in it, you are rendering the best possible service in pointing them out. If the report in the main is a fair and clear presentation of the South's needs, however, small errors of detail surely are of minor importance. That it is fair and clear I am led to believe by the overwhelming volume of favorable editorial comment in the Southern newspapers, and by the statements of leaders in the business, social, and political life of the South. As for alleged errors of detail, I am leaving the discussion of that to some of those men who helped prepare the report. Attached to this letter is their memorandum.

Finally, let me say that whether or not you share the President's view that the South is "the nation's No. One economic problem," I have little doubt that he shares your feeling that the South is "the nation's No. One economic hope."

In any case, I do.

> Sincerely yours,
> (Signed)Lowell Mellett
> The Executive Director

Memorandum on the Letter of Mr. Fitzgerald Hall, President of the Southern States Industrial Conference, Concerning the NEC Report on the Economic Conditions in the South

We can agree with Mr. Hall's statement that the South is the Number One Economic Hope of the Nation. We think the Report consistently indicated this fact. At the same time, however, the Report reveals conditions which, if not remedied, may dissipate or destroy this hope.

While certain statistics may be distorted to present a picture of the

South which omits its problems, no such methods can erase the poverty, the ill health, the undernourishment, the living conditions, and the exploitation evident to the eyes of Southerners and strangers alike.

The South is the Nation's Number One Economic Hope because there is reason to believe the people of the South will use their immense natural resources to raise their average income to heights consonant with modern needs, to free themselves from the drudging poverty of cash cropping, to end the insecurity inherent in the present system of land tenure, to educate all their citizens, to procure every decency, every benefit, and every economic good which wealth of resources makes possible.

It cannot fairly be said that an accurate inventory of the problems of the South holds it up to ridicule and shame, the less so since this inventory was undertaken specifically with the intention that it result in improvements—"that something be done about it." The Report is not an indictment, but simply a summary of facts that can be used as a starting point in seeking solutions.

The assertion that the material "deals largely in generalities such as might be applied to almost any other section of the United States with a similar concentration of population, degree of urbanization, and diversification of industry" is accurate textually but misleading by implication. It is precisely the fact that no other section of the country does have a similar concentration of population, degree of urbanization, and diversification of industry which makes the South's problems peculiar to it, and the description not general but specific.

Thus for example, Mr. Hall criticizes the Report because it uses averages depressed by the low living level of the 29 percent of the South's population which happens to be Negro. While it is true that the standard of living and the income of Negroes wherever they live in the United States is low, it is likewise true that there is no section in the country where Negroes are so numerous as in the South. Merely stating that this 29 percent of the South's population is Negro does not in any way mitigate the fact that this very large number of southern citizens are living under subhuman conditions. And the Negro has no monopoly on poverty in the South.

Mr. Hall asks why the report did not bring out the fact that the median income for white nonrelief village families in 1935 was higher in the Southeast than in most sections of the country. It would have been equally as irrelevant to have brought out the fact that there are some southern millionaires. These village statistics apply to a small, selected group of southern families. The greater part of the South's population as indicated by the studies of rural areas where most of the South's population lives, gives an utterly different picture.

The second objection is equally far from the mark. The ability of a family to add to its net worth on a relatively low income is perhaps commendable, but when it is understood that this addition to net worth is made at the expense of healthy diet, and is made by families that are largely without any of the amenities of present-day living, then the statistics simply become another testimonial to the fact that living levels are abnormally low in the South. Does Mr. Hall argue that since the majority of southern families are without bathrooms, without running water, without proper diet, without any of the common decencies, that these lacks should be used to justify lower incomes, and that the deprivations should continue?

Without questioning the statistics quoted in points 3 and 4 of Mr. Hall's statement, they seem to be selected not to picture conditions in the South as they actually exist but rather to establish a technical refutation of some of the Report's statements. He uses statistics, for example, on the average number of hours worked to prove that the work week in the South is shorter than in other regions—an utterly different matter. The fact that the average number of hours worked per month in the South during 1935 was lower than for the North and the West is more properly a measure of Southern underemployment than an indication of the length of the work day or work week. The statistics compiled by Mr. Hall's association, while no doubt accurate, appear to be a better index of part-time employment, than of the number of hours in the average Southern work week.

On the other hand, in point 4, by pulling out and weighing isolated statistics, which were used in the form of a general average in point 3, he proves, by legerdemain, facts that have no existence in the work-life of Southern industrial employees.

Actually, however, there is ample statistical confirmation for the disparity between the hours of work and the earnings of workers in the North and in the South. "In each district (of the South) wages in the industry of that district," *The Monthly Labor Review* states in an article on wages and hours of labor, "were generally lower than wages in those industries in the North. On the average they were 12.8 percent lower in the Southwest, 13.7 percent lower in the upper South, and 18.4 percent lower in the lower South." The statistics are based on data compiled for 1933 and 1935, the same study to which Mr. Hall referred. Earnings, as distinguished from wages, have always tended to show even greater disparity.

As for hours, the article states, "National averages, however, conceal significant underlying differences. Thus the average of nearly 50 hours a week in manufactured ice (213.1 man-hours per month) does not reflect prevalent practice in the industry. In the North the average approximates 47 hours per week and in the South 53 hours. So also in meat-packing the national average of 175.2 hours per month is an intermediate figure between 173.2 in the North and 188.4 in the South, corresponding roughly to 40 and 44 hours per week."

The same tendency to justify conditions by elaborate statistical rationalization is shown in point 5 of Mr. Hall's statement. The Report's statement on industry was intended only to reveal that the capitalization of industry in the South, its equipment, and its general developmental stage was behind that of the North. No attempt was made to compare the relative generosity of Northern and Southern employers, which aside from being irrelevant, would be presumptuous—even if there were statistical criteria for generosity. The statistics cited, as well as those cited in the Report, indicate only that there is relatively less machinery used per employee in the South than in the North. That fact is important since it bears upon the productivity of Southern industry as compared with Northern industry.

There is no possible statistical method for obscuring the actual condition, yet Mr. Hall cavils at the statement that the South leads the nation in the employment of children in industry. Obviously it is possible to conceal the extent of child labor by computing percentages based upon the relationship between the number of children in factories and the total number of persons in both rural and urban areas. But if accuracy and not concealment is desired, a more proper index may be obtained by comparing the number of child laborers with the number of persons actually employed in factories.

With regard to the statement on freight rate differentials, it is true that variations in rates exist for each of several thousand different commodities. The Report did not attempt to go into specific cases, but simply noted the existence of the problem. The percentage statement was arrived at by the use of index numbers and it may be that further study will modify the specific figures cited. However, notwithstanding he is president of a railroad, Mr. Hall will not quarrel with the conclusion that Southern industry has been unfairly damaged by the present freight rate structure.

On point 8: The report did not intend to minimize the achievements of those industries in the South which, despite the many disadvantages and disabilities that had to be overcome, nevertheless have won a share of the Nation's markets. As noteworthy as this achievement has been, however, no one maintains seriously that Birmingham steel is not shipped north for the manufacture of finished goods which are then reshipped for sale in the South. Perhaps certain fabricating plants in the South are adequate to fill some Southern needs. The tragedy is that these apparent needs are diminished so drastically by the inability of the South to buy what it actually needs. Moreover, despite the contention that some Southern fabricating plants are adequate to some of the South's needs, much of the steel used to reinforce the roads leading to Birmingham today was manufactured in the Pittsburgh-Youngstown area. The locomotives that haul freight and passengers along Southern railroads were manufactured in the North, and the Southern farmer tills his soil with Northern plows. Southern industrialists will not claim that Southern industry has reached the technical development and the volume of production and sales which the South requires so urgently.

As for the question, "Is Pennsylvania or the South the Nation's Number One Economic Problem," which is asked after citing WPA expenditures in the two areas: If it is asked seriously to correct a disparity, then the attempt to represent the South as a community of well paid, well fed, well clothed, well housed, and well cared-for people with no social problems is certainly no proper brief for WPA funds.

The total number of dollars spent on the WPA program in Pennsylvania and in the eleven Southern States has been about the same during the periods from July 1936 through June 1938. However, in making comparisons of this kind, other recovery and emergency programs which the Federal Government has aided should not be ignored. A highly industrial State, such as Pennsylvania, would require more relief from industrial unemployment than a less developed State. During the period from 1933 through December 1937 the Federal Government expended or lent through the Agricultural Adjustment Administration, Farm Security Administration, Rural Electrification Administration, Farm Credit Administration, and the Commodity Credit Corporation, a total of $6,179,000,000. Thirty percent of this amount was disbursed in the eleven Southern States cited by Mr. Hall, whereas less than one percent was expended in Pennsylvania.

THE RESOLUTIONS COMMITTEE

Southern Liberals Respond to the Report:
The Southern Conference for Human Welfare
Birmingham, Alabama

November 20 – 23, 1938

Mr. Clyde Mills of Georgia, Chairman.

Mr. Mills: "Madam Chairman, reporting for the Resolutions Committee, I feel it is desirable we make a short statement explaining why we have asked permission to report on some resolutions before we adjourn for lunch. We realize there are a great number of people who probably would like to go home. We have a mass of resolutions here that look staggering, but we will try to get through as quickly as possible. We have two or three resolutions which the Committee felt were of major importance to this Conference, so we are going to present them and we will adjourn for lunch at any time you make a motion."

Here follows the various resolutions submitted by the resolutions committee, and compiled by them from the various resolutions adopted by the different sections. Where two or more sections submitted resolutions of an identical nature, the resolutions committee combined the sense of the several and drafted a covering resolution. They are tabulated to facilitate time and position. In the words of Raymond Gram Swing, "Our principle findings are offered not as final and incontrovertible, but rather as authentic, informative and suggestive."

Dies. "Resolved: That the Southern Conference for Human Welfare record its condemnation of the procedure employed by the Dies Committee[3] and further condemns its obvious use of Congressional investigatory power to discredit the present administration."

The Resolutions Committee of the Southern Conference for Human Welfare, *Report of Proceedings . . . Birmingham, Alabama, November 20 – 23, 1938)* (n.p., n.d.), 13 – 23.

[3] The U.S. House of Representatives established the House Committee on Un-American Activities (HUAC) in 1938; its chair was Martin Dies, a conservative Democrat from Texas, the sort of southern Democrat who by 1938 was increasingly turning against the New Deal and working with the Republicans. The HUAC almost immediately launched a series of highly public hearings into "subversive" activities by the left, focusing on New Deal agencies and on powerful New Deal allies such as organized labor. These hearings were precursors to the more famous Congressional hearings on Communist subversion held in the later "McCarthy era."

Unity of labor. "Resolved: That the Southern Conference for Human Welfare endorse the efforts of President Roosevelt to promote the unity of the labor movement as expressed in his letters to the AF of L and the CIO Conventions."

Segregation. "Resolved: That the action of Birmingham City Officials in enforcing existing segregation ordinances, as affecting sessions of this conference, demonstrates a situation that we condemn, and be it further Resolved: that this Conference instructs its officers in arranging future meetings to avoid a similiar situation, if at all possible, by selecting a locality in which the practices of the past few days would not be applied."

Wagner Act. "The Resolutions Committee recommends that this conference record itself as opposed to any amendments to the Wagner Labor Relations Act, as now in effect."[4]

Interracial. A Composite report of all resolutions of the Panel of Interracial Groups was submitted by the Resolutions Committee.

> "To achieve full rights and privileges of American citizenship for all people under the law;
> To urge the positive extension of the franchise to all our citizens of proper educational qualifications, in primaries and general elections;
> To urge the abolition of poll-taxes as a prerequisite to voting;
> To endorse and support federal and state anti-lynching legislation;
> To oppose the practice of wage differentials between racial groups;
> To recommend that appropriations for public education be based upon school populations and that we give encouragement to every effort for adult education for all racial groups;
> That interracial meetings in the future be characterized by sincerity, understanding, and intelligence;
> To recommend that adequate appropriations be made by the states for Negro graduate work in Southern state-supported Negro institutions."

[4] The National Labor Relations Act (the Wagner Act), passed in 1935, set up legal machinery to determine whether or not workers wished to bargain collectively with an employer through a union; sharply restricted anti-union practices by employers; and established an independent agency, the National Labor Relations Board (NLRB), with broad discretionary powers of enforcement. The Act was generally regarded by employers as unconstitutional, and the NLRB as stacked in favor of organized labor. After the Supreme Court declared the Wagner Act constitutional in 1938, employers attempted to amend it to curb NLRB powers and generally tilt the balance of power in labor relations back toward management.

Freight rate differentials. "Resolved: That the Southern Conference for Human Welfare go on record as supporting the personal efforts of the Governors of the South, to eliminate in every way possible the discriminatory freight rates which have been imposed upon the South, and we appeal to the people of the South and of the whole nation to give their active support to these efforts."

At this time the Chair asked the Chairman of the Resolutions Committee to postpone any further reading until a short recess had been taken. During this time the Chair announced the names of the Nominating Committee.

Myles Blanchard, Fla.	Wm. M. Minton, Va.
Yelverton Cowherd, Ala.	Father Cullen, Ala.
Forrester Washington, Ga.	Roy Ledbetter, Ark.
Anna H. Settle, Ky.	

The States thereupon met in caucus during the recess, to reconvene at 2 P.M.

Afternoon Session of General Session

The Chair recognized Mr. Clyde Mills, Chairman of the Resolutions Committee.

Mr. Mills continued:

Wages and hours for women. "It is recommended by this Conference that standards already set for women be safeguarded so they cannot be lowered or repealed and that the states extend their laws for women wage earners, shortening hours and extending the coverage of existing hour laws; enacting hour laws where none now exist, and enacting minimum wage legislation for women."

Scottsboro boys. "Resolved: That the Southern Conference requests the Governor of Alabama to exercise his power of executive clemency for the release of the remaining five Scottsboro prisoners."

Farm tenancy. Mr. Mills: The Farm tenant question was discussed and a considerable number of resolutions have been presented by that panel to us; a very voluminous outline of their conclusions. I believe they were [thoroughly] discussed and understood by those who took part in that panel. All of us had an opportunity to either oppose or support this proposed legislation, and in view of that we will recommend that this entire program be referred to the Executive Committee of this Conference to carry out the purposes inaugurated in all resolutions approved by that panel. I move that that be done. In brief, their program is as follows: Resolved: (1) That appropriations to the Bankhead-Jones Farm Tenant Act be expanded to serve a larger number of families; (2) To aid the FSA to expand its program to further supply credit needs and eliminating high rates of interest; (3) That the FSA program of group medicine be continued and expanded; (4) That the co-operative program of the FSA be continued and expanded and that voluntary co-operatives be encouraged; (5) That the FSA establish a supplemental farm ownership program for trained young farmers; (6) That a legal aid bureau for the rural areas be provided by the Federal government [through] an appropriate agency; (7) That a rural program for a subsidized federal housing plan be established similar to the low-income housing plan for cities; (8) That the federal government co-operate with the states in equalizing educational opportunities; and be it further Resolved: That to protect tenants and farm owners [through] state action that (a) agriculture leases be in writing; (b) tenants be encouraged to improve properties by permission to remove all improvements capable of [removal] or to receive a reasonable compensation for same; (c) records be kept of accountings for rent, supplies, and advances; (d) minimum standards of housing and sanitation be provided by the owner; (c) landlords be compensated for all reasonable and proven damage by tenants; (f) differences be settled between owner, sharecropper, or tenant by a committee of arbitration selected by both sides; (g) the right of both owner and tenant be safeguarded by adequate state legislation; and be it further

Resolved: That the Department of Agriculture through appropriate agencies in co-operation with the state agriculture colleges intensify and expand courses of studies regarding the economic, social and legal aspects of farm tenancy.

Poll tax. "Resolved: That the Southern Conference for Human Welfare go on record for (1) the enactment of federal and state legislation to establish uniform registration laws; (2) the elimination of the poll-tax as a prerequisite of voting, both in party primaries and general elections, and (3) liberalization in the election laws of the several states with respect to the requirements for printing the names of parties and independent candidates on the ballot."

Wage differentials. "Recommend[ed]: That the Southern Conference for Human Welfare actively and persistently support the enactment and enforcement of laws relating to the elimination of Home Work; liberalization of Compensation Laws; State laws similar to the Wagner Labor Relations Act, The Fair Labor Standard[s] Act; and adequate Civil Service Laws to guarantee qualified personnel and tenure of office for all Government and State employees charged with the enforcement of the above recommended laws and regulations.

That the Conference express opposition to any wage differential because of geographical or other factor, either in public or private employment."

Eviction of workers. "Resolved: That eviction or the threat of eviction of employees from company-owned houses shall be condemned by the Southern Conference for Human Welfare, as a means of threats, coercion or intimidation on the part of mill owners or managers to prevent the right of workers to organize and bargain collectively, or to avoid rulings and elections held under the auspices of the NLRB."

Women's Bureau. "It is recommended that a Women's Bureau be established in each State Department of Labor, and the active opposition to discrimination in any form based upon the sex of the worker."

Seamen's relief. "It is recommended that this Conference lend all possible aid to secure adequate relief for seamen unemployed because of the tying up of their ships and who are denied relief because of their employment in shipping."

Human rights. "Resolved: That the Conference express its opposition to and disagreement with the interpretations of the 13th, 14th and 15th amendments to the Constitution by the Supreme Court, which placed property rights above human rights, contrary, in our opinion to the intentions of the framers of those amendments."

LaFollette Committee. "Resolved: That there is a need for the continuation of the LaFollette Civil Liberties Committee, and that the Southern Conference for Human Welfare urge the Congress of the United States to make adequate financial appropriations for the continuance of this Committee."

American Bar Association. "Resolved: That this Conference commend the actions of both the American Bar Association and the National Lawyer's Guild in creating agencies designed to protect the civil rights and liberties of the people."

WPA. "Recommend[ed]: That this Conference express its opposition to any wage differentials on WPA projects because of geographical or other factors, and seek the highest possible wage in every locality consistent with public interests."

Public Defender. "Recommend[ed]: That this Conference approve the establishment of the office of Public Defender in every locality where necessary; that the WPA be called upon to set up a lawyer's project to provide legal aid bureaus to serve such portions of the population as cannot secure the services of adequate counsel."

Education. "Recommend[ed]: That the Southern Conference for Human Welfare endorse the principles and provisions of the Harrison-Thomas-Fletcher Bill for Federal Aid to the states, for education, and urge our Representatives in Congress to support this Bill in all its provisions for adult and workers' education, teachers' training, rural libraries as well as public schools.

That the members of this Conference work tirelessly to secure an increase in Federal funds for education in the South.

That the Conference use all its efforts to secure a tax on incomes, particularly on incomes now exempt, those of absentee owners of our industries and resources, for the purpose of elevating our standards of education in comparison with other parts of the country.

That the Conference [through] its Continuance Committees study the problems of making the schools of this Southern region serve more specifically the needs of our people.

That the Southern Conference affirm its belief that a free educational system is a necessary basis for the development and preservation of a democracy."

Credit. "Resolved: That the Southern Conference for Human Welfare favors the future development of the South's resources for the benefit of the South by the reduction of interest rates, both for industrial and farm credit;

That the Conference further favors the expansion of Federal credit facilities either through Regional Banks or through an insurance fund guaranteeing long time loans made by existing private banks."

WPA munitions. "Resolved: That this Conference condemn any proposal to force WPA workers into munition factories and urge the extension of projects which will contribute to the cultural, constructive, and social well-being of the people."

Social Security. "Be it Resolved: That the Southern Conference for Human Welfare endorse the principle of the Social Security Law, including old age pensions provisions, and urge the enforcement and extension of these provisions to include those groups not now covered, together with adequate collateral legislation by the states."

Sales tax. "Resolved: That this Conference request each legislature of the South to pass graduated income tax laws; and that all sales taxes be repealed forthwith."

Housing. "Resolved: That the Southern Conference endorse the housing and slum clearance program of the Federal Administration, and urge additional appropriations sufficient to extend its scope to meet the real needs of the South; and urge Southern members of Congress to introduce such legislation."

Congress of Mexican and Spanish-American Peoples. "Resolved: That this first Southern Conference for Human Welfare endorse the 'First Congress of the Mexican and Spanish-American Peoples of the United States' to be held in Albuquerque, New Mexico, on March 24, 25, and 26, 1939."

Prison reform. "We Recommend: that this Conference express its support of laws adequate to provide protection to juvenile delinquents; the establishment of a broad system of playground and recreation centers; the elimination of political consideration from prison, parole, and probation administration; improvement [through] Federal aid in sanitary standards in prisons; to provide a more diversified and constructive system of vocational training in penal institutions with a proper safeguard for workers in private employment by limiting the sale of prison-made articles to the State; approve an intelligent application of the system of parole; making provision for future strengthening and proper understanding of the parole problems by development of professional instruction in this field of social welfare in our colleges."

Seven Acts. Mr. Mills at this point introduced a series of proposed acts to be introduced in the various State Legislatures. The Committee Recommended approval of the principle embodied in the act proposed but not in the letter of the Act. These acts were summarized briefly, and presented with the recommendation they be referred to the Executive Committee:

(a) A Bill proposed to prevent and to alleviate to some degree the trouble we find in the States, in cases of injunctions issued in labor disputes.

(b) An Act dealing with the use of privately paid deputy sheriffs calling attention to the abuse of that practice and proposing a Bill to be introduced preventing that practice in the States.

(c) Another Act providing for the protection and guarantee of civil liberty, prohibiting interference with parades or meetings in or on public streets and in public places, except as specifically provided, providing for the full and equal protection of all.

(d) An Act providing covenants to be introduced in contracts for the purchase of supplies and materials entered into by the State or agencies thereof.

(e) An Act relating to the payment of wages by employers to employees by requiring the employer to pay wages to employees at least twice a month and to advise the employee of the date of such payment; to pay wages due when employees are discharged, resign, or become involved in industrial disputes; to be responsible for wages due to employees of subcontractors of the employers; to maintain records; authorizing the Secretary of Labor to accept assignments of wage claims and to institute civil proceedings therefor; prescribing penalties; and repealing inconsistent Acts.

(f) An Act licensing and regulating private detectives, private police, and private guards; prescribing penalties and repealing inconsistent Acts.

(g) An Act to protect rights of employees to organize and bargain collectively and to create a Labor Relations Board in each State as an extension of the Wagner Labor Relations Act by the Federal Government into the States.

Freedom of speech. "Resolved: That this Conference express its unalterable support for a free press, free speech, and free assembly, as the foundation for a democracy, and condemn the practice of influencing the judgment of people through the publication by newspapers of propaganda supplied by organizations established for that purpose, and urges that the LaFollette Committee particularly investigate further the propaganda subsidies of great corporate wealth which threaten the freedom of the press."

Peace. "Resolved: That this Conference express its vigorous condemnation of the persecution of religious groups by Nazi Germany and other

European Countries, and that we commend President Roosevelt's action in expressing the indignation of the American people, and Be it further Resolved: that we endorse an American peace policy such as proposed by President Roosevelt and Secretary of State Hull, to promote the national security of our country, to curb aggression, and assist the democratic peoples of the world to preserve peace, liberty, and freedom."

Birth spacing.   "The Southern Conference for Human Welfare recommends the inclusion of birth spacing clinical service in the public health agencies of the Southern States."

Youth problems.   Mr. Mills: We have a rather broad statement of desires and proposals in relation to the question of youth, especially in the Southern States. We do not believe we could go far enough to act on each and every one of them. One of the resolutions referred to the establishment of a Youth Council within this organization of the Southern Conference. We recommend that this be done, and that the program drawn up by the Youth Section of this conference be referred to the Executive Committee to carry out so far as may be possible the principles included in the Youth Section's report, which are briefly summarized as follows:

(a) That the Southern conference express its appreciation for the valuable contributions of the NYA and the CCC in meeting the needs of southern young people.

(b) That it endorse the Southern Advisory Committee's recommendation for the establishment of a Federal Youth Service Administration combining the programs and administrations of NYA and CCC under civilian control.

(c) That it urge increased appropriations to more adequately meet the needs of students and unemployed youth.

(d) That it favor the establishment of student co-operatives.

(e) That long-term loans at low rates of interest be made available to farm youth.

(f) That increased funds be provided for vocational and technical training in schools and colleges for both rural and urban youth.

Child labor.   "Resolved: That this Conference endorse the Child Labor provision of the Federal Fair Labor Standards Act and that necessary Federal and State legislation be enacted to secure adequate enforcement of the Child Labor provisions of this Act. That State Legislation be enacted to supplement the Federal Act by covering intrastate occupations; that completion of ratification of the Federal Child Labor Amendment to the

Constitution of the United States by all Southern States which have not so ratified.

Public health.   The following resolutions were presented by Mr. Mills with the explanation that owing to the shortness of time which had elapsed since the Public Health Section had closed its session, they had not been considered by the complete Resolutions Committee, but which he presented for approval by the General Session.

(a) A recommendation that in view of the fact that in many counties of the Southern States there are no physicians and dentists, and that in many more counties these services are inadequate, that provision be made for medical service and dental and institutional service for the low-income groups in rural areas.

(b) Recognizing that the medical, dental, and institutional care of the indigent is woefully inadequate, and is a social responsibility, that this Conference recommends the expansion of governmental technical and financial aid in medical, dental, and institutional care.

(c) That qualified Negro physicians be granted an opportunity to render professional service to Negro patients in tax-supported institutions.

Playground facilities for Negroes.   A resolution from the housing Section calling attention to certain conditions existing in Birmingham in regard to the inadequacy of playground and recreational facilities for Negroes and resolving that this Conference recommend to the Federal Government that it include in the Housing and Slum Clearance projects adequate playground and recreational facilities to combat juvenile delinquency, crime, immorality, poor health, human misery, and undue governmental expense and that this Conference urge the Federal Government to construct such a playground and recreational facility for the Negro youth of Birmingham according to the data, plans, and estimates of costs as drawn up by the representatives of the Birmingham Public Schools."

N.E.C. report.   *Mr. Mills:*   Before I go into this following resolution I wish to express the sentiments of the entire Resolutions Committee for the establishment of this Conference and of the possibility of good that may come out of it. I do not believe we can be too strong in our expressions of gratitude to the members of the Southern Advisory Committee for their splendid work on the report on Economic Conditions in the South. It is not a biased report, but an honest attempt to paint the actual picture as they found it and in painting it to the devoted concern not only of the South but the nation as a whole. Therefore it is with a great deal of appreciation I submit this:

"Resolved: that this Conference go on record as thanking the President of the United States for calling to the attention of the National Emergency Council, the South as 'the Nation's number one Economic Problem' and providing means whereby this problem could become known, recognized, and corrected in so far as we are able. And,

Be it Further Resolved: That we commend the Southern Advisory Committee on Economic Conditions in the South for the concise and analytical report on the fifteen subjects they so thoroughly treated. We further thank all those who contributed to the compilation of this Report."

Thanks. Mr. Mills: I personally move the following: "That we extend our thanks and appreciation for the manner in which we have been received; for the manner in which the various agencies which will be named, have co-operated in carrying out or assisted us in carrying out the purposes for which this Conference was called, and I move that we extend our thanks and a vote of appreciation to the Churches of this city, to the Auditorium staff, to the Hotel Tutwiler, to the Press, to the Police Department, to the Women's Civic Club, to the City Commission and to all State and Federal Departments who constructed exhibits."

Each of the above resolutions was moved and duly seconded that it be adopted upon its presentation by Chairman Mills. After the completion of his report as Chairman, the entire report was adopted by the General Session upon proper motion and second. Whereupon Mr. Daniels of Texas moved that the Resolutions Committee be thanked by the Conference for its labor, and that the permanent committees of the Conference consolidate and simplify the resolutions and give them whatever publicity possible. This was duly seconded, voted upon, and passed. It was moved and seconded from the floor that the complete proceedings of the conference be printed and that copies be made available to all delegates at the lowest possible cost and that copies be sent to every legislator in the thirteen Southern States, and all members of Congress from the Southern States.

Mr. Wm. Mitch, Vice-Chairman, who was presiding at this time, recognized Mrs. Anna H. Settle, of Louisville, Kentucky, reporting for the Nominating Committee. Mrs. Settle submitted the names for officers of the Executive Committee of the Southern Conference, and the names of members of the Southern Council. Upon motion from the floor, Dr. Frank P. Graham was nominated for Chairman. Mrs. Charlton asked for the privilege of making Dr. Graham's election unanimous, but this being voted down, the session proceeded to ballot, electing Dr. Graham, Chairman, and electing Carl Thompson of Raleigh, N.C., to take Dr. Graham's place as vice-chairman from North Carolina, and Mr. C. A. Wilson of North Carolina to substitute for Mr. Thompson as one of the seven members from North Carolina on the Southern Council. There being no further corrections nor nominations, Mrs. Settle moved that the Secretary be instructed to cast one ballot for the nominees on all the remaining offices, which was so ordered.

Thereupon it was moved and seconded from the floor that the Conference establish another office entitled "Honorary Chairman of the Southern Conference for Human Welfare." This carried, thereupon Mrs. Louise Charlton was unanimously elected to such office. A motion being made and seconded from the floor that Dr. H. C. Nixon be appointed Executive Secretary, which was voted upon and carried. Mrs. Charlton resumed the chair, and in closing said: "There is a motion to adjourn before the house, and I crave your indulgence for a moment before putting that motion. I thank you from the bottom of my heart for giving me the privilege of serving under Dr. Frank Graham. It is customary, I believe to give the retiring officer a silver service, but you have done far more — you have given me a Golden Treasure, and I thank you, as I said before, from the bottom of my heart. There being no further business to come before this Session of the Southern Conference for Human Welfare, I, your retiring Chairman, hereby declare it adjourned."

Suggestions for Further Reading

Biles, Roger. *The South and the New Deal.* Lexington: University Press of Kentucky, 1994.

Cobb, James C. *Industrialization and Southern Society, 1877 – 1984.* Lexington: University Press of Kentucky, 1984.

Cobb, James C., and Michael V. Namorato, eds. *The New Deal and the South: Essays.* Jackson: University Press of Mississippi, 1984.

Couch, W. T., ed. *These Are Our Lives.* Chapel Hill: University of North Carolina Press, 1939.

Danhof, Clarence H. "Four Decades of Thought on the South's Economic Problems," in Melvin L. Greenhut and W. Tate Whitman, eds., *Essays in Southern Economic Development.* Chapel Hill: University of North Carolina Press, 1964, 7 – 68.

Daniel, Pete. *Breaking the Land: The Transformation of Cotton, Tobacco, and Rice Cultures since 1880.* Urbana: University of Illinois Press, 1985.

Davis, Steve. "The South as 'The Nation's No. 1 Economic Problem': The NEC Report of 1938," *Georgia Historical Quarterly* 62 (Summer 1978): 119 – 132.

Dorman, Robert L. *Revolt of the Provinces: The Regionalist Movement in America, 1920 – 1945.* Chapel Hill: University of North Carolina Press, 1993.

Egerton, John. *Speak Now Against the Day: The Generation before the Civil Rights Movement in the South.* New York: Alfred A. Knopf, 1994.

Johnson, Gerald W. *The Wasted Land.* Chapel Hill: University of North Carolina Press, 1937.

Krueger, Thomas A. *And Promises to Keep: The Southern Conference for Human Welfare, 1938 – 1948.* Nashville: Vanderbilt University Press, 1967.

Mertz, Paul E. *New Deal Policy and Southern Rural Poverty.* Baton Rouge: Louisiana State University Press, 1978.

O'Brien, Michael. *The Idea of the American South, 1920 – 1941.* Baltimore: Johns Hopkins University Press, 1979.

Odum, Howard W. *Southern Regions of the United States.* Chapel Hill: University of North Carolina Press, 1936.

Reed, Linda. *Simple Decency and Common Sense: The Southern Conference Movement, 1938 – 1963.* Bloomington: Indiana University Press, 1991.

Schulman, Bruce J. *From Cotton Belt to Sunbelt: Federal Policy, Economic Development, and the Transformation of the South, 1938 – 1980.* New York: Oxford University Press, 1991.

Singal, Daniel Joseph. *The War Within: From Victorian to Modernist Thought in the South, 1919 – 1945.* Chapel Hill: University of North Carolina Press, 1982.

Sosna, Morton. *In Search of the Silent South: Southern Liberals and the Race Issue.* New York: Columbia University Press, 1977.

Terrill, Tom E., and Jerrold Hirsch, eds. *Such as Us: Southern Voices of the Thirties.* Chapel Hill: University of North Carolina Press, 1978.

Tindall, George B. *The Emergence of the New South, 1913 – 1945.* Baton Rouge: Louisiana State University Press, 1967.

———. *The Ethnic Southerners.* Baton Rouge: Louisiana State University Press, 1976.

Vance, Rupert B. *Human Geography of the South: A Study in Regional Resources and Human Adequacy.* Chapel Hill: University of North Carolina Press, 1932.

Wright, Gavin. *Old South, New South: Revolutions in the Southern Economy since the Civil War.* New York: Basic Books, 1986.

(Acknowledgments continued from page ii)

Mary Hicks and Walter Harrison. Reprinted from *These Are Our Lives,* Federal Writers' Project, Regional Staff. Copyright © 1939 by the University of North Carolina Press. Used by permission of the publisher.

Lowell Mellett. Letter to Fitzgerald Hall, September 19, 1938. Frank Porter Graham Papers, Series 1.1, 1938, Folder 71.

Ida Moore. Reprinted from *These Are Our Lives,* Federal Writers' Project, Regional Staff. Copyright © 1939 by the University of North Carolina Press. Used by permission of the publisher.

Howard W. Odum. Reprinted from *Southern Regions of the United States.* Copyright © 1936 by the University of North Carolina Press. Used by permission of the publisher.

Walter Rowland. Reprinted from *Such as Us: Southern Voices of the Thirties,* edited by Tom E. Terrill and Jerrold Hirsch. Copyright © 1978 by the University of North Carolina Press.

PHOTO CREDITS

Figs. 1 – 4 (pp. 83 – 87) are reproduced from the Collections of the Library of Congress.

Index

CPSIA information can be obtained at www.ICGtesting.com
Printed in the USA
267895BV00003B/2/P